I0458952

# Septuagint:

# Deuteronomy

## Septuagint, Volume 5

Scriptural Research Institute
Published by Digital Ink Productions, 2024

# COPYRIGHT

While every precaution has been taken in the preparation of this book, the publisher assumes no responsibility for errors or omissions, or for damages resulting from the use of the information contained herein.

**Septuagint: Deuteronomy**

Second edition. February 18, 2024

Copyright © 2024 Scriptural Research Institute

ISBN: 978-1998636600

The Septuagint was translated into Greek at the Library of Alexandria between 250 and 132 BC.

This English translation was created by the Scriptural Research Institute in 2019 through 2024, through the comparison of most published copies of Septuagint manuscripts. Additionally, the Leningrad Codex, Aleppo Codex, Peshitta, targums, Shapira Scroll, and the Dead Sea Scrolls were used for comparative analysis.

The image used for the cover is "Moses Descending the Mountain" by Raven Mahikan.

# TABLE OF CONTENTS

# TABLE OF CONTENTS

# TABLE OF CONTENTS

# FORWARD

In the mid-3<sup>rd</sup> century BCE, King Ptolemy II Philadelphus of Egypt ordered a translation of the ancient Hebrew scriptures for the Library of Alexandria, which resulted in the creation of the Septuagint. The original version, published circa 250 BCE, only included the Torah, or in Greek terms, the Pentateuch. The Torah is the five books traditionally credited to Moses, circa 1500 BCE: *Cosmic Genesis*, *Exodus*, *Leviticus*, *Numbers*, and *Deuteronomy*.

The English name *Deuteronomy* is a corruption of the Greek Deuteronómion (Δευτερονόμιον), which means "secondary law." This suggests it was originally in circulation as an series of amendments to the Torah. However, it covers the same ground as *Leviticus* and *Numbers*, indicating it was used by a different priesthood from the Yahwists of Libnah, likely a priesthood that only acknowledged the laws in *Names* (*Exodus*). The Hebrew version of the book is known as Dəbārîm (דְּבָרִים), which translates as "Words." The oldest surviving complete copy of Words is found in the Leningrad Codex, which dates to 1008 or 1009 CE. Chapters 32 through 34 of the Aleppo Codex's Names also survive, which date to circa 920 CE. Fragments of Names have been found among the Dead Sea Scrolls, which date to between 165 BCE and 400 CE. The majority of these fragments were written in Hebrew, however a couple of the fragments were in older Phoenician script.

1

The earliest complete copies of the Septuagint's *Deuteronomy* date to the 4$^{th}$ and 5$^{th}$ centuries CE, and are found in the Vaticanus, Colberto-Sarravianus, Alexandrinus, and Ambrosiano A 147 codices. Fragmentary older copies of *Deuteronomy* exist, including the three fragments of the Papyrus Fouad 266, which date to the late 2$^{nd}$ or early 1$^{st}$ century BCE. Additionally, copies of *Deuteronomy* survive among the Peshitta, Vetus Latina, Vulgate, and Coptic manuscripts dating to earlier than the Aleppo Codex. Several Aramaic targums also originated around the time of the Septuagint, however, the oldest surviving manuscripts date to after the Aleppo Codex.

It is generally accepted that there were several versions written in Aramaic and Canaanite dialects before the translation of the Septuagint. Fragments of the Torah have been found in four languages among the dead sea scrolls, generally dated to between 200 BCE and 600 CE. During this time, the land of Judea passed from the rule of the Ptolemys in Egypt to the rule of the Seleucids in Syria around 200 BCE. The Seleucids attempted to Hellenize the Judeans, erecting a statue of Zeus in the Second Temple in Jerusalem, and effectively banning traditional Judaism. This Hellenizing activity was partially successful, creating the Sadducee faction of Judaism, however also led to the Maccabean Revolt in 165 BCE, which itself created the independent Hasmonean Kingdom of Judea.

This kingdom was violently xenophobic and led by a priestly monarchy that combined both the powers of the state and the church. The Hasmonean dynasty attempted to conquer all of the territory that had previously been part of the Persian Province of Judea, and either evicted or exterminated the people that were living there, depending on their ethnicity. When the Edomites were conquered they were allowed to mass-convert to Judaism as they were considered the descendants of Esau, however, most other ethnic groups were not welcome. When the army of Hasmonean King John Hyrcanus annexed Samaria in 113 BCE, he slaughtered the Samaritan priests and more than half the Samaritan population and enslaved the rest. His army also destroyed the Samaritan Temple on Mount Gerizim and burned all copies of their holy books. The Samaritans continued to be slaves under the Hasmoneans until the Roman General Pompey's armies freed them in 69 BCE, and restored the independent state of Samaria, along with several other states that fell under Rome's protection from that time forward.

The Hasmoneans blamed the Greeks for all of Judea's problems and attempted to forge an alliance with the Roman republic. The Hasmoneans appear to have promoted Yahweh Sabaoth partially in order to forge closer ties with the Romans, as Yahweh (Iaw) was pronounced very similar to Jupiter (Iove). The Romans did not respond well to this, and threw the Jews out of Rome in 139 BCE, as recorded by Valerius Maximus:

*"Gnaeus Cornelius Hispalus, praetor peregrinus in the year of the consulate of Marcus Popilius Laenas and Lucius Calpurnius, ordered the astrologers by an edict to leave Rome and Italy within ten days, since by a falla-*

*cious interpretation of the stars they perturbed fickle and silly minds, thereby making profit out of their lies. The same praetor compelled the Judeans, who attempted to infect the Roman custom with the cult of Jupiter Sabazius, to return to their home."*

While the Hasmoneans ruled Judea, they converted the national script from the old Phoenician script, today called Paleo-Hebrew, to the Aramaic "block script," today called Hebrew. As a result, almost all surviving texts found from the Hasmonean era and later are written in the Aramaic script, and it is unclear how much the Hasmoneans redacted the scriptures when they transcribed them. The scriptures the Hasmoneans left the world were later used as the basis of the Masoretic texts, which is used today by Rabbinical Jews, as well as by Catholic and Protestant Christians.

The Samaritan Torah is believed to have been restored after General Pompey freed the Samaritans, by redacting a copy of the Hasmonean Torah, which is why there are fewer differences between the Samaritan and Jewish Torahs than the either of them and the Septuagint. A copy of the original Samaritan Torah was translated at the Library of Alexandria as well, referred to as the Samareitikon (Σαμαρειτικον), however, it has not survived to the present. Based on the writings of Origen of Alexandria in the early 3$^{rd}$ century, and other early Christians, the Samareitikon was more similar to the Septuagint's Pentateuch than it was to either the Samaritan or Jewish Torahs in use at the time.

The differences between the Masoretic texts and the Septuagint are both minor and startling, as the two sets of scriptures contain the same stories, but different Gods. The Masoretic version of *Deuteronomy* was mostly about the actions of Yahweh, Yahweh Elohim, Yahweh Sabaoth, or Elohim, while the Septuagint contains the Greek translations of various gods' names that appear to have been redacted by the Hasmoneans. The God of the book of Genesis in the Septuagint is called Lord the god (Κυριοσ ο θεοσ), or simplified to Lord (Κυριοσ), or God (Θεοσ). These terms are mirrored in the Masoretic texts by Yəhōwâ 'ĕlōhîm (יְהוָה אֱלֹהִים), Yəhōwâ (יְהוָה), and 'ĕlōhîm (אֱלֹהִים), respectively.

The explanation for these differences is found in the Masoretic Book of Daniel, which was only partially translated into Hebrew, leaving about half of the book in Aramaic, transcribed into the Assyrian script. The Aramaic sections of Masoretic Daniel that were not translated into Hebrew maintain the term 'ădōnāy hā'ĕlōhîm (אֲדֹנָי הָאֱלֹהִים), meaning "lord of the gods" where the Septuagint has "Lord the god" (Κυριον τον θεον), however, the Hebrew sections have Yəhwâ 'ĕlōhîm (יְהוָה אֱלֹהִים) where the Septuagint has "Lord the god," suggesting the Greek more accurately reflects the Aramaic source texts than the Hebrew translation.

According to records from the time, this was to repair the damage King Manasseh had done 600 years earlier when he removed the name of god from the Israelite texts, which is reported in the Sanhedrin (103b) tractate in the Talmud, however, Manasseh's grandson King Josiah published a "restored" version of the Torah around 628 BCE, and therefore, if the name was originally in the text, he would have restored it. The name that Manasseh actually cut from Hezekiah's Torah, appears to have been Šadday (שַׁדָּי), as the name continues to exist in the Leningrad Codex's Bereshít, Names, and *Numbers*, however, all references to Shaddai are entirely missing from Septuagint's translations of *Cosmic Genesis*, *Exodus*, and *Numbers*, indicating it wasn't in the Egypto-Aramaic version the Greeks translated.

The name Yahweh, transliterated into Greek as Iaō (Ιαω) from its Egypto-Aramaic form of Yǻw (𐤉𐤀), was originally been in some of the books of the Septuagint, such as *Leviticus*, which originated under the rule of King Josiah, and Yahweh was a popular god among Judeans and Egypto-Israelites under Persian and Greek rule. Under the Hasmonean Dynasty, it was added to all the books translated into Hebrew, creating some confusion among early Christians.

There were debates in the early Christian era about which version of the Israelite scriptures to use, the Greek, Hebrew, Samaritan, or Syriac translations, resulting in different versions of the scriptures being used by different churches. Some versions replaced the name Lord with Iaō in the Greek texts, either in the Greek form as Ιαω, or by copying in the Hebrew form of the name Yhwh (יהוה) or the older Phoenician form of Yhwh (𐤉𐤄𐤅𐤄), or by mocking the Hebrew with Greek letters as ΠΙΠΙ. This created a great deal of confusion among Christians, and ultimately the books of the Septuagint that had the name Iaō in them were redacted so all

the books used the term Lord (Κυριοσ). Most Christian translations, as well as Jewish translations, have continued to use the
term "Lord" in place of the name Yahweh, due to the prohibition on using any names of God that was introduced during
the Hasmonean dynasty.

The terms in *Deuteronomy* are translations of known
Canaanite gods, most especially, El, the Canaanite creator-god.
El translates in Canaanite and Hebrew as "God," and is the
primary god worshiped in ancient Canaan in the era Abraham
was reported to have passed through the area. If the Greeks
translated the Septuagint accurately, which everything other
than the names of God indicates, then the term God (Θεοσ)
would have been Ål (ᒐᴎ) in the texts they translated.
Likewise, Lord the god (Κυριοσ ο θεοσ) would have been
ådny hålwhym (ᒐ^ᴎᒐᴎ ᴧᒐᴎ), the title of El, which translates as "Lord of the gods," and Lord (Κυριοσ) would have
been ådny (ᴧᒐᴎ), meaning "my lord." El was also the patron
god of the Temple of El, built by Jacob near the modern city
of Nablus in the Palestinian West Bank, which featured in
many of the early Hebrew scriptures before Samaria was
conquered by the Assyrian Empire. In the Book of Micah, the
Temple of El was referred to as Jacob's Temple of El, which
confirms that the Israelites in the 8th century BCE considered
the Temple of El at Shiloh to be the Temple of El that Jacob
built, in *Cosmic Genesis* and Bereshít chapter 35.

The word ål (אל), meaning "god," is used throughout the
Septuagint, but generally in relation to other gods, or as a part
of a name, such as Israel, or Beth-El, proving El was of

primary importance throughout the early era of the Israelite religion, before they adopted Iaw. There is an exception in *Deuteronomy*, where the word God (Θεου) in the Septuagint is mirrored by El (אֵל) in the Masoretic Text, and in both texts appears to be a proper name. This example is in the Song of Moses, in chapter 32:

> *You have forsaken the God that fathered you and forgotten El who feeds you.*

The Song of Moses in chapter 32 describes the Lord as being one of God's messengers, the one who received the Israelites as his portion when God divided the children of Adam among the messengers. In Second Temple era literature, the patron messenger of the Israelites was Gabriel, while the patron messenger of the Persians was Dobiel. There is a story in the Talmud that dates back to the Persian era which explains the rise of the Persian Empire instead of an Israelite Empire. In this story, when the Persians occupied Babylonia, God wanted the Israelites in Babylon to be sacrificed, however, Gabriel took pity on them and let them return to Judea. God punished Gabriel and removed him from office for 21 days, during which time Dobiel filled in, and he caused the rise of the Persian Empire. This belief in the national messengers did not die out when the Second Temple was destroyed, as Dobiel and Samiel were described as the national messengers of the Persians and Romans when the *Revelation of Metatron* was written, which is broadly dated to between 100 and 1000 CE.

The Septuagint's book of *Deuteronomy* has what appears to be a reference to Moses praying to Lord Hadad, king of the gods, in chapter 2, which would imply that he was the Lord of *Deuteronomy*, while later in chapter 10, the Leningrad Codex version of *Deuteronomy* has the Lord stating his "name is Shamayim" (וּשְׁמֵי הַשָּׁמָיִם). Hadad and Shamayim were both Canaanite gods which King Josiah banned during his religious reforms, circa 625 BCE. Hadad was more commonly known as Ba'al at the time, however, is called Hadad, his proper name, in modern history books in order to distinguish him from the many other Canaanite gods referred to by the title Lord (Ba'al). The text in which Lord Hadad is possibly identified in the Septuagint is entirely missing in the Masoretic texts, which supports the fact that the Hasmoneans considered it contrary to their religious views. This title of the Lord in the Septuagint was:

*Lord Lord king of gods (Κυριε Κυριε βασιλευ των θεων)*

If this was translated correctly from the Aramaic source text, then the verse read:

*Lord Ba'al king of the gods (५^תLN१ NJL१ NL"१ ५१N)*

In the ancient Canaanite Ba'al Cycle, from between 1400 and 1200 BCE, Lord Hadad became the king of the gods after defeating Lord Yam (Sea) and Lord Mot (Death), and gaining the support of the other 70 children of El. It is clear that the Ba'al Cycle was in use among the Judeans during the time of King Josiah, as the prophet Jeremiah quoted it, however, this sentence goes directly against the reforms of Josiah, who explicitly and vehemently banned the worship of Ba'al in *4ᵗʰ Kingdoms* (Masoretic Kings) chapter 23:

> *The king commanded Hilkiah the high priest, and the priests of the second order, and those that kept the door, to bring out of the temple of Ba'al all the vessels that were made for Ba'al and Asherah, and all the army of Shamayim, and he burnt them outside of Jerusalem in the fields of Kidron, and took the ashes of them to the Temple of El. He burnt the sacred male prostitutes, who the kings of Judah had appointed, (they burnt incense in the bamahs and in the cities of Judah, and the places around Jerusalem), and they who burnt incense to Ba'al, and Shemesh, and Yarikh, and the Zodiac, and the army of Shamayim.*

> *He carried out the Asherah from the Temple of of the Lord to the brook Kidron, and burnt it at the brook Kidron, and reduced it to powder, and threw its powder on the sepulchers of the sons of the people. He pulled down the Palace of Qetesh that was by the Temple of the Ba'al, where the women wove tents for the Asherah. He brought up all the priests from the cities of Judah and defiled the bamahs where the priests burned incense, from Geba all the way to Beersheba.*

> *He pulled down the house of the gates that were by the door of the gate of Joshua the ruler of the city, on a man's left hand at the gate of the city. The priests of the bamahs did not go up to the altar of Ba'al in Jerusalem,*

*for they only ate leavened bread with their brothers. He defiled Tafeth which is in the valley of the son of Hinnom, constructed for a man to cause his son or his daughter to pass through the fire to Moloch. He burnt the horses which the king of Judah had given to Shemesh in the entrance of the Temple of Ba'al, by the treasury of Nathan the king's eunuch, in the suburbs, and he burnt the Chariot of Shemesh with fire.*

*The altars that were on the roof of the upper room of Ahaz, which the kings of Judah had made, and the altars which Manasseh had made in the two courts of the Temple of Ba'al, the king pulled down and forcibly removed from there, and threw their dust into the Brook of Kidron. The king defiled the temple that was near Jerusalem, on the right hand of the mountain of rubbish, which Solomon king of Israel built to Astarte the abomination of the Sidonians, and to Chemosh the abomination of Moab, and to Moloch the abomination of the Ammonites. He broke in pieces the steles, and completely destroyed the groves, and filled their places with the bones of men. Also the high altar in Bethel, which Jeroboam the son of Nebat, who made Israel sin, had made, even that high altar he tore down, and broke in pieces the stones of it, and reduced it to powder, and burnt the grove.*

*Josiah turned aside, and saw the tombs that were there in the city, and sent, and took the bones out of the tombs, and burnt them on the altar, and defiled it, fol-*

*lowing the word of law which the prophet spoke...*

This description of the destruction of the temples of the Canaanite gods makes it clear that neither the Lord's identification as Hadad or Shamayim would have been acceptable under Josiah's rule, which indicates that *Deuteronomy* was either not written yet, or was in use among the Samaritans, outside of Judea at the time. The reference to Shamayim found in the Masoretic version of *Deuteronomy* does not flow in the text and appears to have simply been added by a Shamayim-worshiping scribe, which would indicate it was in use in Samaria under Assyrian rule. Based on the Book of Jonah, the Canaanite god Shamayim was regarded as the local variant of Asshur, the national god of Assyria, who by that time was known as Ansar (⊬⊲), meaning the "Whole Sky." Jonah claimed that he was a prophet of Shamayim, the god of his owner, when he went to Nineveh, which was the only reason the Assyrians would have listened to a runaway slave.

The authorship of *Deuteronomy's* laws can also be placed outside of Judah by the book's treatment of qədēšâ (קְדֵשָׁה) and qādēš (קָדֵשׁ) in chapter 23, which the Greeks translated as "healers" (τελεσφόροσ) and "initiates" (τελισκόμενοσ). The kadesh are the sacred male prostitutes that King Josiah executed, however, *Deuteronomy's* laws simply state that Israelites may not allow their children to become qədēšâ and qādēš, implying the practice itself was fine, but only for lesser races. There are a number of Second Temple era texts that stipulate that Israelites may not be prostitutes, yet are accepting of other ethnic groups being prostitutes, which this verse seems to be implying. *Deuteronomy's* laws certainly do not state "slaughter the qədēšâ and qādēš," just "don't let your children become qədēšâ and qādēš." The two terms, qədēšâ and qādēš, are both related to the worship of Qetesh, whose palace in Jerusalem was destroyed by King Josiah. Qetesh was the title of Asherah, as well as several other goddesses in Canaan and Mesopotamia, and a significant amount of research and debate has gone into the development and history of the cult.

The qādēš were the sacred male prostitutes of the Temple of Qetesh, however, modern scholarship doubts the translation prostitute is accurate, as they did perform sexual acts, but did not get paid, and so the term "sex-worker" is generally used in academic literature. The cult itself goes back to Sumeria, as the cult of Inanna, which in Sumerian mytho-history originated in the land of Aratta, long before the time of Sumeria. Throughout most of its history, the sex-workers were male, however, the descriptions indicate they were either transvestites or transgender, depending on the local customs regarding castration.

The qədēšâ, which is sometimes translated as female prostitutes, were in most cases nuns that worked at the palace, and do not appear to have engaged in sexual relations with men, as they were the sacred property of the goddess. This sex-cult was widespread from the Sumerian era, before 3000 BCE, through the Akkadian, Babylonian, Assyrian, Hittite, and Mitanni civilizations. Under Persian rule, the position of eunuchs changed and they began to be hired by the Imperial

government to fill bureaucratic positions because it was
believed they were less likely to be corrupted by greed, as
they had no children to leave their possessions to. This seems
to have resulted in the cult having increasing amounts of
female prostitutes before it finally died out under Greek rule.
Some smaller groups did survive, as documented by the
Romans when they conquered Anatolia.

Any of the references to Ba'al, Shamayim, or Qetesh seem
out of place in a book used under Josiah's rule, and the fact
that all three appear to be present, two mentioned explicitly
in the Masoretic version, and one implied by the Septuagint,
indicates that *Deuteronomy* could not have been in use in
Judah at that time. All three of the deities in question were
worshiped in Samaria, both before it fell to Assyrians, and
under Assyrian rule, and therefore, *Deuteronomy* is likely
Samaritan in origin. *Deuteronomy* retells or mentions various
stories from the first four books of the Torah, and adds a
secondary set of laws, intended to supplement the laws in the
book of *Exodus*. The name *Deuteronomy* (Δευτερονόμιον)
means "Second Law," while the Hebrew name is Dəbārîm
(דְּבָרִים), meaning "Words," suggesting the book may have
circulated independently from the Torah before Ezra united
them circa 351 BCE.

The retelling of the stories found in *Leviticus* and
*Numbers* seems to be a parallel tradition, and not simply
restating what was already written, implying some version of
*Deuteronomy* may be older than *Leviticus* and may have
even been one of the sources used when *Numbers* was

compiled under Josiah. Many of the terms used in *Deuteronomy* imply it is older, and likely a collection of laws from the Kingdom of Samaria, however, in chapter 24 the author explicitly states to follow the laws regarding leprosy that the Levites will provide, and to remember what happened to Mariam. This is a clear reference to the books of *Leviticus* and *Numbers*, which indicates that *Deuteronomy's* text was still being added to in the Babylonian era.

Chapters 29 and 30, the Curse of Moses, and the promise of forgiveness certainly appear to have been written after the Assyrians conquered Samaria in 720 BCE, as they promise that after the Israelites have been spread through the nations, even to the ends of the earth, if they repent, they will be restored to the promised land. This is an odd thing for Moses to have said as the Israelites were preparing to invade Canaan, but, is a great addition to the Torah when the Israelites have been taken as slaves to the far reaches of the Assyrian Empire. It is equally possible that this line was added later, during the Babylonian era, as they took away Judahites as captives, and in either case, it would indicate that *Deuteronomy* was used by the Samaritan priesthood that became dominant in Babylonian Judah.

The Samaritan priesthood was thrown out of Jerusalem by Ezra the Scribe circa 351 BCE, who is credited in the Talmud as rewriting the Torah, as it had been lost when the Babylonians destroyed Jerusalem. However, the Samaritan priesthood had to have had a Torah, and Ezra most likely just redacted it to fit the requirements of the priesthood he was creating. Some have theorized that he wrote *Deuteronomy*, however, that seems unlikely as he would not have been so lenient towards the qədēšâ and qādēš, and certainly would not have included the sentences that indicate Hadad and Shamayim were considered the Lord when sections of *Deuteronomy* were written. It is possible that he added the Curse of Moses, and the promise of forgiveness, however, by his time the Judahites were already free to return, and so the promise would have been pointless.

A series of wars including both Julius Caesar's campaigns, and a Parthian invasion led to the weakening of the Hasmonean dynasty, and in 37 CE, the Roman Senate appointed Herod the Great as King of the Jews. Herod's rule wasn't particularly popular, as he allowed the Romans to establish themselves within Judea, however, he did expand Judea, reintegrating the Greek and Samaritan cities, and annexing Galilee and Edom. When he died, his kingdom was divided between four successors, a situation that ended in 66 CE when the Romans conquered the region. An uprising in 120 CE led to the Jews being exiled from Judea, and the region became a Greco-Roman colony. In the wake of the Jews, the Samaritans rose in numbers, along with the Christians once Christianity was legalized. Between 529 and 555 CE, the Samaritans revolted and were effectively annihilated, by Constantinople the Eastern Roman capital.

The ancient documents found in the Caves in Qumran, more commonly called the Dead Sea Scrolls, span most of Judean history. The fragments of the Torah have been found in ancient Phoenician, Hebrew, Aramaic, and Greek. The Phoenician fragments in the dead sea scrolls have been particularly debated, as they are believed to be the oldest. The current Hebrew script was adopted by the Jewish intelligentsia during the Babylonian captivity, however, their ancestors during the time before the Babylonians conquered them used the Phoenician script. Multiple dialects of Canaanite were written in this script, including Samaritan, Judahite, Edomite, Moabite, Ammonite, and Sidonian. The Samaritans never stopped using the ancient Phoenician script, and it continued to develop over time into the modern Samaritan script.

The modern Samaritan religion is similar to Judaism, in that they have versions of the Torah and the *Book of Joshua*, however, they do not trace their ancestry to ancient Judah, but rather to ancient Samaria also called the Northern Kingdom of Israel. According to the Samaritans, they were the original Israelites, and the Temple of Yahweh was not Solomon's Temple in Jerusalem, but rather a Temple on Mount Gerizim, in Samaria. These "other Israelites" also contributed to the creation of the Septuagint, as the Book of Tobit, was the story of a Samaritan that had been taken to Nineveh, the capital of the Assyrian Empire after the Kingdom of Israel was conquered by the Assyrians. This book and several others were not considered important to Simon the Zealot, and not translated into Hebrew.

Outside of Judea, the Septuagint was the dominant form of Israelite scriptures across the Greek-speaking world, which at the beginning of the Christian era extended from the Roman Empire in the west, to the Indo-Greek Kingdom in the east. Judean traders had established small colonies along the trade routes of the Red Sea and the Indian Ocean, reaching as far south as Eritrea, and as far east as southern India, and these Judeans spoke Aramaic and Greek and used the Septuagint. The earliest Christians used the Septuagint exclusively, as far as the Israelite scriptures were concerned, and as a result, it is impossible to even understand the chronology of the world they described unless using the Septuagint. It is unclear why the Septuagint, Masoretic texts, and Samaritan Asatir each contain a different chronology of the world. Adding the Book of Jubilees, and various variations of the Torah found within the Dead Sea Scrolls, there are no less than six ancient Israelite chronologies.

The *Cosmic Genesis* includes an additional millennium of human history that was dropped from Bereshít in order to align the creation of the world with the beginning of the age of El, when the constellation Taurus became the marker of the northern vernal equinox, in 3760 BCE. The Bull El was the dominant God of the Canaanite pantheon until circa 1700 BCE, when Attar the Goat (Aries) and Yam the Sea-Monster (Cetus) fought for domination of the world beneath the sky, ultimately both being replaced by the god of thunder Ba'al Hadad, in the Canaanite Ba'al Cycle. Traditional Jewish interpretations of the timeline within the Masoretic texts, is further hampered by the so-called "missing years" of Rabbinical Time, in which hundreds of years of the Persian Empire are skipped over in order to make the timeline fit into the era since 3760 BCE, a problem Christian chronologists have never had as Christianity developed after the astrology of Babylonian-era Judaism had been forgotten.

The earliest Bibles, all used the Septuagint, however, by the 4th century some Christian scholars were asked whether they should retranslate the Old Testament from the version the Jews were using, and some even suggested using the Samaritan version. Both suggestions were generally dismissed as heretical, as Jesus and the Apostles had quoted from the Septuagint, even though they had access to the Hebrew version then in use. This argument held in the west until the Middle Ages, when Catholic Bibles switched to the Masoretic Text. In the east, Orthodox Bibles continued to use the Septuagint, as they do today. To the south, the Ethiopian Tewahedo Church continued to use the Septuagint, and across Asia, the Thomas Christians and Nestorians continued to use the Septuagint. Only in Western Europe were the later Masoretic texts adopted, abandoning the more ancient Septuagint, on the assumption that the Jews had copied their texts more faithfully than the Greeks had translated them. This assumption was carried forward into the Protestant Churches that broke off from the Catholic Church, and therefore almost all Protestant Bibles use the Masoretic Text for the basis of the Old Testament.

Unfortunately, this means that the earliest Christian writing is generally confusing and ignored by Protestants and Catholics. The earliest Christians of the first and second centuries quoted books that are no longer in the Bible, and as such, their writings are not always understood. Septuagint: *Deuteronomy* is the fifth in a series of 21st century translations aimed at correcting this problem. *Septuagint: Deuteronomy* also maintains the old wording of the Song of Moses, which relates that the Highest divided the nations of man, he awarded the children of Jacob to the Lord, and the other nations to other messengers, which indicating that the Lord was once seen as a messenger, and not God himself.

One of the problems with academic translations of the Septuagint, is the use of unfamiliar names or terms, as the Septuagint was in Greek, and therefore many names are unrecognizable to modern readers. This project uses the more commonly understood Hebrew-derived names instead of their Greek translations, such as Canaan instead of Chanaan, and Melchizedek instead of Melchisedec. Common modern names are also used instead of either Greek or Hebrew terms when geographical locations are known, such as the archaeological name Uruk instead of the Greek Orech, or the Hebrew Erech, and the archaeological term Sumer instead of Shinar or Senar. While this could be argued as not being a correct academic procedure, it does fulfill the goal of making the translation easy to read and understand.

# CHAPTER 1

These are the words that Moses[1] said to all of Israel on this side of the Jordan in the desert towards the west near the Sea of Edom,[2] between Paran,[3] (and Meson),[4] Tophel,[5] and Laban,[6] and Aulon,[7] and the gold works.[8] It is a journey of eleven days from Horeb[9] past Mount Seir[10] to Kadesh Barnea.[11] In the fortieth year, in the eleventh month, on the first day of the month, Moses spoke to all the children of Israel and told them all the things which the Lord[12] commanded him for them. After he had destroyed Sihon king of the Amorites who lived in Heshbon, and Og the king of Bashan who lived in Ashteroth and Edrei.

Beyond Jordan in the land of Moab, Moses began to declare this law, saying, "the Lord of the gods[13] spoke to us in Horeb, saying, 'Let it be enough for you to live so long in this mountain. Turn and leave, and enter into the mountain of the Amorites, and go to all that live near Arabah,[14] to the mountain and the plain and to the south, and the land of the Canaanites near the sea, and Anti-lebanon, as far as the great river, the river Euphrates. See, delivered before you is the land, go in and inherit the land, which I swore to your fathers, Abraham, Isaac, and Jacob, to give it to them and to their descendants after them."

I said to you at that time, "I will not be able to bear you by myself. The lord of the gods has multiplied you, and, Look, today you are as many as the stars in the sky. The lord of the gods of your fathers increased you a thousand-fold more than you are and bless you as he has said to you. How will I alone be able to bear your labor, and your burden, and your disputes? Give to yourselves wise and understanding and prudent men from your tribes, and I will set your leaders over you."

You answered me, "That which you have told us to do is good."

So I took from you wise and understanding and prudent men, and I set them to rule over you as rulers of thousands, and rulers of hundreds, and rulers of fifties, and rulers of tens, and scribes to your judges. I ordered your judges at that time, "Hear cases between your brothers and judge rightly between a man and his brother, and the stranger that is with him. You will not have respect to a face in judgment, you will judge equally between small and great. You will not shrink from before the person of a man, for the judgment is God's. Whatever matter will be too hard for you, you will bring it to me, and I will hear it.

I ordered you at that time all the commands which you will perform. We departed from Horeb, and went through all that great and terrible wilderness, which you saw, by the way of the mountain of the Amorite, as our lord of the gods ordered us, and we came as far as Kadesh Barnea. I said to you, "You have come as far as the mountain of the Amorite, which our lord of the gods gives to you. Look, the lord of the gods has delivered to us the land ahead of you. Go in and inherit it as the lord of the gods of your fathers said to you. Don't be afraid, nor be fearful."

You all came to me, and said, "Let us send men before us, and let them go up to the land for us, and let them bring back to us a report of the way by which we will go up, and of the cities into which we will enter."

The suggestion pleased me, and I took of you twelve men, one man per tribe. They left and went up to the mountain, and they came as far as the valley of the cluster and surveyed it. They took in their hands of the fruit of the land, and brought it to you, and said, "The land is good which our lord of the gods gives us."

Yet you would not go in but rebelled against the words of our lord of the gods. You murmured in your tents, and said, "Because the Lord hated us, he has brought us out of the land of Egypt to deliver us into the hands of the Amorites, to destroy us. To what place do we go?"

Your brothers drew away your heart, saying, "It is a great nation and populous, and mightier than we, and there are cities great and walled up to the sky. Moreover, we saw there the sons of the Anaks."[15]

I said to you, "Don't be afraid, or be fearful of them, the lord of the gods ahead of you. He will fight against them together with you effectually, according to all that he worked for you in the land of Egypt, and in this wilderness which you saw, by the way of the mountain of the Amorite. How the lord of the gods will carry you like a nursling, like any man would nurse his child, along all the way which you have traveled until you have come to this place. In this matter you did not believe our lord of the gods, who goes before you along the way to find you a place, guiding you in fire by night, showing you the way by which you go, and a cloud by day."

The Lord heard the sound of your words, and being greatly provoked he swore, "Not one of these men will see this good land, which I swore to their fathers, except Caleb the son of Jephunneh. He will see it, and to him, I will give the land on which he went up, and to his sons, because he obeyed closely the will of the Lord."

The Lord was angry with me for your sake, saying, "Neither will you by any means enter there. Joshua the son of Nun, who stands by you, he will enter in there. You strengthen him, for he will cause Israel to inherit it. Every young child who this day knows not good or evil, they will enter there, and to them, I will give it, and they will inherit it."

You turned and marched into the wilderness, in the road along the Papyrus Sea. You answered and said, "We have sinned before our lord of the gods. We will go up and fight according to all that our lord of the gods has commanded us, and having taken everyone his weapons of war, and being gathered together, you went up to the mountain."

The Lord said to me, "Tell them, 'You will not go up and fight, for I am not with you, so you will not be destroyed before your enemies."

# CHAPTER 1

I spoke to you, and you did not listen to me, and you transgressed the commandment of the Lord, and you forced your way and went up into the mountain. The Amorites who lived in that mountain came out to meet you and chased you like bees do, and slaughtered you from Seir to Hormah. You sat down and wept before our lord of the gods, and the Lord did not listen to your voice, neither did he pay attention to you. You lived in Kadesh many days, as many days as you lived there.

## CHAPTER 1 NOTES

**1** Codex Vaticanus: Mōusēn (ΜѠΥϹΗΝ)

• LXX 58: Mōsēs (Μοοϩⲥ)

• Leningrad Codex: Mosheh (מֹשֶׁה)

• Shapira scrolls: Mšh ôl py Yhwh (𐤅𐤄𐤉 𐤆𐤋 𐤋𐤏 𐤔𐤌). Translation: Moses from (in Samaritan, or 'on top of' in Judahite and Hebrew, 'on the head' in Akkadian and Babylonian) mouth of Yhwh

• Peshitta: Mwšå (ܡܘܫܐ)

• Targum Onkelos: Mosheh (מֹשֶׁה)

• Fragment Targums: Mosheh (מֹשֶׁה)

• Targum Pseudo-Jonathan: Mosheh (מֹשֶׁה)

• Codex Lugdunensis (LV 100): Moyses ex ore domini (ⲘOYSES EX ORE ꝺOⲘINI). Translation: Moses from the lord

• Sahidic manuscript 296L: Mōusēs (ΜⲱΥϹΗϹ)

It is generally accepted that at some point before the Septuagint was translated, half of Moses' name was redacted from the text. This theory is based on the similarity of the Egyptian term msỉ (𓄹𓏤),

meaning "give birth to," or "created by," which was a common element of Egyptian names. Many kings of Egypt were known as the "msi" of a god, including Ramses (𓇳 𓄟𓇋𓇋), Ahmose (𓄿𓄟𓇋𓇋), Tuthmose (𓅱𓄟𓇋𓇋), Amenmose (𓇋𓏠𓈖 𓄟𓇋𓇋), and Ptahmose (𓁹 𓄟𓇋𓇋𓊪). A theory that has been circulating since at least the time of Josephus in the 1ˢᵗ century CE, is that Moses' original name was Hapymoses, meaning the 'Nile created him.'

If this is the origin of the name, the name of the god that created Moses was likely dropped from the name very early in Israelite history, as there are no known surviving texts with the full name. The latest this is likely to have happened would have been during the Aramaic translation of King Hezekiah, however, it may have happened much earlier.

An alternate interpretation is that the name is complete, and is derived from the Egyptian term mw-šåȯ (𓈗𓈖𓈘𓈘), meaning 'beginning on water,' which appears to be what the princess stated in *Exodus*, when she found Moses and named him.

**2** Codex Vaticanus: en tē erēmō pros dusmais plēsion tēs Eruṭras (ЄΝ ΤΗ ЄΡΗΜω ΠΡΟC ΔΥCΜΑΙC ΠΛΗCΙΟΝ ΤΗC ЄΡΥΘΡΑC). Translation: in the undefended (or abandoned, void, lonely) towards west near Erythras (or Red)

• Septuagint manuscript 407: en tē erēmō pros dusmas plēsion tēs Eruṭras (ου τη βλημω περς Δυσμας πλησϊ𐅁 ϱ͂ βυθϱας). Translation: in the undefended (or abandoned, void, lonely) towards west near Erythras (or Red)

• Septuagint manuscript 121: en tē gē erēmō pros dusmais plēsion tēs Eruṭras (ου τη γη βλημω περς Δυσμαις πλησϊ𐅁 ϱ͂ βυθϱας). Translation: in the land undefended (or abandoned, void, lonely) towards west near Erythras (or Red)

# CHAPTER 1

- Septuagint manuscript 58: en tē erēmō pros dusmais plēsion tēs Erutras talassēs (ⲟ ⲧⲏ ⲣⲏⲙⲱ ⲡⲣⲟⲥ Ⲇⲩⲟⲙⲁⲓⲥ ⲡⲗⲏⲟⲧⲟ ⲧⲏ ⲣⲩⲑⲣⲁⲥ Ⲑⲁⲗⲗⲟⲟⲏⲥ). Translation: in the undefended (or abandoned, void, lonely) towards west near Erythras (or Red) Sea

- Leningrad Codex: bammidbār bā'Ărābâ môl Sûp (בַּמִּדְבָּר בָּעֲרָבָה מוֹל סוּף). Translation: in the wilderness of Arabah (or plain, desert) opposite (or against), facing Sup (or papyrus, reeds)

- Shapira scrolls: bmdbr bôbr hyrdn bôrbh (𐤁𐤌𐤃𐤁𐤓 𐤁𐤏𐤁𐤓 𐤄𐤉𐤓𐤃𐤍 𐤁𐤏𐤓𐤁𐤄). Translation: in the wilderness beyond (or across) the Jordan in the plain (or Arabah). This verse suggests the Shapira scrolls was written in Samaria or Judah, not Moab, where it was supposedly discovered.

- Peshitta: bmdbrâ bôrbâ lwqbl swp (ܒܡܕܒܪܐ ܒܥܪܒܐ ܠܘܩܒܠ ܣܘܦ). Translation: in the wilderness in the west (or Arabah, guardian, groomsman, ram, sheep, lamb, sunset, guarantee) facing Swp (or papyrus, reeds)

- Targum Onkelos: bəmadbərā' wə'al də'argîzû bəmêšərā' loqŏbēl yam Sûp (בְּמַדְבְּרָא וְעַל דְּאַרְגִּיזוּ בְּמֵישְׁרָא לְקֳבֵל יַם סוּף). Translation: in the wilderness and at the snake (or serpent) of correction (or rectitude, uprightness) opposite the sea of Sup (or papyrus, reeds)

- Targum Jerusalem: Mšeh wa'ămar ləhôn hălā' bəmadbərā' bətûrā' dəSînay 'ityəhîbat ləkôn 'ôrayytā' ûbəmêšərā' dəMô'āb 'itparšat ləkôn kammâ nisîn ûgəbûrān 'ābad ləkôn mêmərā' daYyā kad hăwêtûn qayymîn 'al yamā' dəSûp (מֹשֶׁה וַאֲמַר לְהוֹן הֲלָא בְּמַדְבְּרָא בְּטוּרָא דְסִינַי אִתְיְהִיבַת לְכוֹן אוֹרַיְיתָא וּבְמֵישְׁרָא דְמוֹאָב אִתְפַּרְשַׁת לְכוֹן כַּמָּה נִסִין וּגְבוּרָן עֲבַד לְכוֹן מֵימְרָא דַיְיָ כַּד הֲוֵיתוּן קַיְימִין עַל יַמָּא דְסוּף). Translation: Moses said to them, "Wasn't it in the wilderness of the Mount of Sinai that was given to you the instruction (or Torah, law), and in the plains (or valleys) of Moab where separated and corrected and tested, but heroes worshiped firmly the command of Yah. When wounded for you at the Sea of Papyrus (or reeds)..."

# CHAPTER 1

• Targum Pseudo-Jonathan: wa'ămar ləhôn hălā' bəmadbərā' bətawrā' dəSînay 'ityəhibat ləkôn 'ôrayytā' ûbəmêšəraya' dəMô'āb 'itparšat ləkôn kammâ nîsîn ûpərîšan 'ăbad ləkôn Qûdəšā' bərîk hû' mizman da'Ăbartûn 'al gêp yamā' dəSûp (וַאֲמַר לְהוֹן הֲלָא בְמַדְבְּרָא בְּטוּרָא דְסִינַי אִתְיְהִבַת לְכוֹן אוֹרַיְיתָא וּבְמֵישְׁרַיָא דְמוֹאָב אִתְפַּרְשַׁת לְכוֹן כַּמָּה נִיסִין וּפְרִישָׁן עֲבַד לְכוֹן קוּדְשָׁא בְּרִיךְ הוּא מִזְמַן דַּעֲבַרְתּוּן עַל גֵּיף יַמָא דְסוּף). Translation: ...and said to them, "Wasn't it in the wilderness of the Mount of Sinai that was given to you the instruction (or Torah, law), and in the plains (or level places) of Moab where explained (or corrected) how many miracles (or camps, libations) and explanations were given from Qûdəšā (or holiness, Qetesh), blessed by He (or she, it), caused for the Abartus (or Oberites) on the shore of the Sea of Sup (or papyrus, reeds)

• Codex Lugdunensis: in solitudine campestri Moab contra mare Rubrum (ɪɴ sᴏʟɪᴛᴜᴏɪɴᴇ ᴄᴀᴍᴘᴇsᴛʀɪ ꟽᴏᴀʙ ᴄᴏɴᴛʀᴀ ꟽᴀʀᴇ ʀᴜʙʀᴜꟽ). Translation: in secluded (or solitude, lonely) countries (or rural lands) of Moab against the Red Sea.

• Sahidic manuscript 296L: terēmos ethnmma nhōtp mprē mpemto ebol ntEruṯra ṯalassa (ⲦⲈⲢⲎⲘⲞⲤ ⲈⲦϨⲚⲘⲘⲀ ⲚϨⲰⲦⲠ ⲘⲠⲢⲎ ⲘⲠⲈⲘⲦⲞ ⲈⲂⲞⲖ ⲚⲦⲈⲢⲨⲐⲢⲀ ⲐⲀⲖⲀⲤⲤⲀ). Translation: in empty (or barren, wilderness) in the abode of the sun (or Ra) in the sky's depths (or face) out of the Eruthra Sea

• Sahidic manuscript 2001: terēmos ethnmma nhōtp mprē mpemto ebol ntEruṯra ṯalassa (ⲦⲈⲢⲎⲘⲞⲤ ⲚⲘⲘⲀ ⲚϨⲰⲦⲠ ⲘⲠⲈⲘⲦⲞ ⲈⲂⲞⲖ ⲚⲦⲈⲢⲨⲐⲢⲀ ⲐⲀⲖⲀⲤⲤⲀ). Translation: in empty (or barren, wilderness) and joins in the sky's depths (or face) out of the Eruthra Sea

The Greek and Hebrew translations differ here, indicating that the Imperial Aramaic translation must have read the same as the Syriac, as in Aramaic, the term ôrbå (עֲרָבָ / ܥܪܒܐ) could be interpreted as either "west" as the Greeks translated, or as "Arabah," as the Hebrew translations reads. The earlier meanings of the word were the Akkadian cuneiform erēbu (𒂊𒊑𒁍), meaning 'to arrive' and Ugaritic ȯrb (𒀭𒊑𒅇), meaning "to enter," suggesting that in the bronze age, the verse referred to the Israelite arriving at the Sea of Papyrus (סוֹף), not being in Arabah, the southern region of modern Israel and Jordan.

Most of the surviving manuscripts do not include the word "sea" (θαλασσης). It is not found in any of the Hebrew or Syriac manuscripts, and only a few Greek manuscripts. It is however, found in the Vetus Latina and Coptic manuscripts, as well as the Targums, indicating that this was the common interpretation by both Jews and Christians in the Roman era.

The Greek name Eruṯras (Ερυθρας) is not geographically specific, and referred to the entire Persian Gulf, Red Sea, and the Indian Ocean. The Greeks were likely referring to the Gulf of Suez, however, this was known to the ancient Egyptians as the "Sea of Calm" (𓏤𓃀𓈖𓏏𓇋𓈖𓏭𓈖𓈖), which is what the Israelites would have called it if that was where they were. The Hebrew translation places the event in the Gulf of Aqaba, however, this was known to the ancient Egyptians as the "Sea of Edom" (𓏤𓃀𓈖𓏏 𓈖𓏏𓂋𓈖) which is what the Israelites would have called it if that was where they were. The Egyptian name is accepted as being adopted from the Canaanite name of the Gulf of Aqaba, which was ym Ȧdm (𐎊𐎎 𐎀𐎄𐎎) in Ugaritic, ym Ȧdm (𐤉𐤌 𐤀𐤃𐤌) in Phoenician, and ymȧ hȦydm (ימא הֱאדם) in Aramaic, all of which translate as "Sea of Edom." As "Edom" and "red" were both spelled as ȧdm (𐤀𐤃𐤌) in Canaanite (Judahite, Samartian, Edomite), and ȧydm (אֱאדם) and Aramaic, the Aramaic texts that the Greeks translated probably used the name Sea of Edom/red, suggesting the Aramaic translator believed that the Sea of Papyrus was the Sea of Edom. Based on the writings of Jeremiah, the Sea of Papyrus was accepted as having been the Sea of Edom by the 7th century BCE. In the 6th century

BCE, Arabs began settling in southern Edom, during the 5th century BCE southern region of Edom bordering the Gulf of Aqaba was annexed by the kingdom of Lihyan. By the 4th century BCE, when the Greeks conquered the Persian Empire, the Gulf of Aqaba was known as the Gulf of Lihyan, meaning the older term "Sea of Edom" no longer made sense, and was interpreted by the Arameans and Greeks as the 'Sea of Red.'

Based on this verse, and the transition of the word ȯrb (〈⚏-Ⅱ〉) in the bronze age, to ȯrbh (ᴣᴣᴎᴑ) in the iron age, it is likely that the Samaritan, Judahite, and Edomite priests and scribes believed that the Sea of Papyrus was the old name of the Gulf of Aqaba, which is at the southern end of the Arabah valley.

The Greeks transliterated the name as the Sea of Sif (θαλασσης σιφ) in the Codex Vaticanus' translation of *Judges*, confirming that the name Swf was in some of the Aramaic text they worked from. The Aramaic term swf (ףוﬡ) and Phoenician term swf (ףﬤﬦ), both meaning 'papyrus plants,' were adopted from the Egyptian term twfi (⬒𓎡𓏏𓈖𓆰), which referred to papyrus, papyrus plants, and papyrus marshes. The Egyptian term continued to be used into the Classical era as the Sahidic word joouf (ϫⲟⲟⲩϥ), and Bohairic words honf (ϭⲟⲛϥ) and homf (ϭⲟⲙϥ), all meaning papyrus. Conversely, the Egyptian name of the Red Sea was the Sea of Heh (𓎛), meaning "very large sea" from the Middle Kingdom era onward, however, it is believed to have originally been named after the ancient Egyptian frog god Heh (𓁫𓎛). In the early Classical era it was also known as the Sea of Ǩôr (ϫⲟⲣ), meaning anger, however, it was never referred to as the Sea of "Papyrus" in surviving Dynastic Egyptian documents. The Hebrew term "sea of papyrus" is not geographically specific either, however, does match the description of the shallow Lake Bardawil which has been a major source for papyrus reeds throughout Egyptian history.

# CHAPTER 1

As there are two "Papyrus Seas" in the Hebrew translation, however, a Sea of Sif (Papyrus) and a Sea of in Eruṭras (Red, Edom) in the Greek texts, the two seas are named either Papyrus Sea or Sea of Edom in this translation, based on their location along the route the Israelites traveled out of Egypt.

**3** Codex Vaticanus: Faran (ⲪⲀⲢⲀⲚ)

- Leningrad Codex: Pā'rān (פָּארָן)

- Peshitta: byt Prn (ܒܝܬ ܦܪܢ). Translation: house (or temple, abode) of Prn

- Targum Onkelos: Pā'rān də'ittappālû 'al mannā' ( עַל דְּאִתְפַּלוּ פָּארָן מַנָּא). Translation: Paran where they insulted the mana

- Targum Jerusalem: madbərā' dəPā'rān (דְפָארָן מַדְבְּרָא). Translation: wilderness (or desert) of Paran

- Targum Pseudo-Jonathan: Pā'rān (פָּארָן)

- Sahidic manuscript 296L: Faran (ⲫⲁⲣⲁⲛ)

- Sahidic manuscript 2001: not mentioned in the verse

- Bohairic manuscripts: Farran (Ⲫⲁⲣⲣⲁⲛ)

The Wilderness of Paran was mentioned in *Cosmic Genesis*, *Numbers*, *Deuteronomy*, and *3rd Kingdoms* (Masoretic *Kings*), and Masoretic *Habakkuk*, however, the location of Paran is debated. *Numbers* states that Paran was Kadesh, while the Masoretic version of *Deuteronomy* locates it in the Arabah Desert of southern modern Jordan and Israel. In the 2nd century CE, the Christian geographer Claudius Ptolemy located it in the southern Sinai Peninsula, at the region now called the Wadi Feiran, while Islamic scholars have interpreted it as the Hijaz region of western Saudi Arabia, around Mecca.

# CHAPTER 1

**4** Septuagint manuscript 118: kai ana Meson (ܟܝ ܐܢܐ ܡܥܣܘ)

The addition of Meson is found in several Greek manuscripts, as well as Arabic translations, and appears to have originated in the Syriac Hexapla.

**5** Codex Vaticanus: Tofol (ⲧⲟⲫⲟⲗ)

- Codex Ambrosiano A 147 (LXX F): Tofel (ⲧⲟⲫⲉⲗ)
- Codex Freer Greek MS. V (LXX W¹): Gofol (ⲅⲟⲫⲟⲗ)
- Septuagint manuscript 509: Tofoa (ⲧⲟⲫⲟⲁ)
- Septuagint manuscript 392: Tofan (ⲧⲟⲫⲁⲛ)
- Septuagint manuscript 58: Tofōl (ⲧⲟⲫⲱⲗ)
- Septuagint manuscript 426: Ṭofol (ⲑⲟⲫⲟⲗ)
- Septuagint manuscript 767: Tofal (ⲧⲟⲫⲁⲗ)
- Septuagint manuscript 55: Tofōn (ⲧⲟⲫⲱⲛ). LXX 55 places Tofōn after Aylōn.
- Septuagint manuscript 761: Tofor (ⲧⲟⲫⲟⲣ)
- Leningrad Codex: Tōpel (תֹּפֶל)
- Peshitta: byt Tpl (ܒܝܬ ܬܦܠ). Translation: house (or temple, abode) of Tpl
- Targum Onkelos: Tappālû (תַּפְּלוּ)
- Targum Jerusalem: not mentioned in the verse
- Targum Pseudo-Jonathan: Təpaltûn (תְּפַלְתּוּן)
- Codex Lugdunensis (LV 100): Hobol (ɦoʙoʟ)
- Sahidic manuscript 296L: Tōfol (ⲧⲱⲫⲟⲗ)
- Sahidic manuscript 2001: not mentioned in the verse
- Sahidic manuscript 2006: Tofor (ⲧⲟⲫⲟⲣ)
- Sahidic manuscript 2178L: Tofol (ⲧⲟⲫⲟⲗ)

**6** Codex Vaticanus: Lobon (ⲗⲟʙⲟⲛ)

# CHAPTER 1

- Codex Ambrosiano A 147: Laban (ܐܐܒܐܢ)
- Septuagint manuscript 16: Lōbon ( λοομⲫ)
- Septuagint manuscript 318: Lobōn (λομοⲟ∾)
- Septuagint manuscript 82: Dobon (ᴅομⲫ)
- Septuagint manuscript 72: Lōbōn (λοομοⲟ∾)
- Septuagint manuscript 59: Labōn (λᴅμⲟ∾)
- Septuagint manuscript 376: Lob (λομ)
- Leningrad Codex: Lābān (לָבָן)
- Peshitta: Lbnn (ܠܒܢ)
- Targum Onkelos: not mentioned in the verse
- Targum Jerusalem: not mentioned in the verse
- Targum Pseudo-Jonathan: not mentioned in the verse
- Sahidic manuscript 296L: Labōn (ⲖⲀⲂⲰⲚ)
- Sahidic manuscript 2001: Lobon (ⲖⲞⲂⲞⲚ)
- Sahidic manuscript 2006: Lobōn (ⲖⲞⲂⲰⲚ)
- Bohairic manuscripts: Lobona (ⲗⲟⲃⲟⲚⲀ)

This location is generally considered unknown, however, based on its generally location, is likely the same place the Egyptians called Rbn during the New Kingdom era, as Egyptians did not distinguish between Ls and Rs like Semitic peoples.

7 Codex Vaticanus: Aulōn (ⲀⲨⲗⲰⲚ)
- Septuagint manuscript 509: Aulon (Ⲁυ/ⲟ∾)
- Septuagint manuscript 528: Auton (Ⲁυⲧⲫ)
- Leningrad Codex: Hăṣērōt (חֲצֵרֹת)
- Peshitta: Ḥṣrwt (ܚܨܪܘܬ)
- Targum Onkelos: not mentioned in the verse

# CHAPTER 1

- Targum Jerusalem: Ḥăṣērôt (חֲצֵרוֹת)
- Targum Pseudo-Jonathan: Ḥăṣērôt (חֲצֵרוֹת)
- Sahidic manuscript 296L: Aulōn (ⲀⲨⲖⲰⲚ)
- Sahidic manuscript 2001: not mentioned in the verse

**8** Codex Vaticanus: Katakrusea (ⲕⲀⲦⲀⲬⲢⲨⲤⲈⲀ)
- Codex Venetus: Katakrusaia (ⲕⲀⲦⲀⲬⲢⲨⲤⲀⲒⲀ)
- Septuagint manuscript 14: Katakruseōn (Κατάχρυσσων)
- Septuagint manuscript 52: Katōkrusea (Κατωχρυσά)
- Septuagint manuscript 58: kata ta Krusea (κατὰ τὰ χρυσά).
Translation: with the gold
- Leningrad Codex: dî zāhāb (דֵּי זָהָב). Translation: enough (of sufficient) gold
- Peshitta: dyzhb (ܗܒܕܙ). Translation: that gold (or coins, money, goldsmith)
- Targum Onkelos: 'ēgal didhāb (עֵגֶל דִּדְהַב). Translation: calf of gold
- Targum Jerusalem: dahăbā' sənînā' (דַהֲבָא סְנִינָא). Translation: golden bush
- Targum Pseudo-Jonathan: 'êgal dahăbā' (עֵיגַל דַהֲבָא). Translation: calf of gold
- Sahidic manuscript 296L: mn Katakrusa (ⲘⲚ ⲔⲀⲦⲀⲬⲢⲨⲤⲀ). Translation: and Katakhrusa
- Sahidic manuscript 2001: Katakrusea (ⲔⲀⲦⲀⲬⲢⲨⲤⲈⲀ)
- Sahidic manuscript 2006: not mentioned in the verse

Based on the general geography described, this "enough gold," was likely the cradle of gold near modern Medina in Saudi Arabia, which was a large gold mining center in Arabia for over 6000 years.

**9** Codex Vaticanus: Ǩōrēb (ⲭⲱⲣⲏⲃ)

- Septuagint manuscript 318: Ǩorēb (χοβλυ)

- Septuagint manuscript 55: Ǩōrib (χοοβιυ)

- Septuagint manuscript 130: Ǩōrēn (χοοβλω)

- Septuagint manuscript 767: Ǩōrēṯ (χοοβλθ)

- Leningrad Codex: Hōrēb (חֹרֵב)

- Shapira scrolls: Ḥrb (Яꜰ𐤄)

- Peshitta: Ḥwryb (ܚܘܪܝܒ)

- Targum Onkelos: Hōrēb (חֹרֵב)

- Targum Jerusalem: ṭûrā' dəHôrēb (טוּרָא דְחוֹרֵב). Translation: mountain of Horeb

- Targum Pseudo-Jonathan: Hôrēb (חוֹרֵב)

- Sahidic manuscript 296L: Ǩōrēb (ⲭⲱⲣⲏⲃ)

Throughout most references to Mount Horeb and Mount Sinai, they appear to be references to the same mountain, both in the Torah, and later in other works, such as *3ʳᵈ Kingdoms* (Masoretic *Kings*). The two names are believed to be derived from the names of the Sun and the Moon. The name Horeb is believed to be derived from the word for glowing/heat, while the name Sinai is derived from the name of the Semitic moon-god Sin. Various Jewish and Christian scholars have tried to resolve the issue of the same stories happening on two mountains. In the Middle Ages, the Rabbi Abraham ibn Ezra suggested that there was only one mountain, with two peaks, while later during the Protestant Reformation John Calvin suggested it was one mountain where the eastern side was named Sinai, while the western side was named Horeb.

Biblical scholars in the 1800s and 1900s developed the alternate hypothesis that two names are derived from two Torah traditions, one Solar and one Lunar, which were then united into a single

# CHAPTER 1

Torah under the rule of King Josiah or earlier. Subsequent theories have suggested the unification of the two Torahs could have taken place later, under the Persian or even Greek rule of Judea, however, it seems unlikely to have happened that late as the Samaritan Torah has virtually identical twin stories about Horeb/Sinai, and the schism between the Jews and Samaritans appears to have happened during the life of Ezra the Scribe, circa 351 BCE. The term Horeb is generally associated with Moses, while Sinai is more often found in texts about Aaron, which implies that whatever the origin of the story, two versions have developed by the time of Josiah, one focused on Moses' Solar-Snake god, and the other focused on Aaron's Lunar-Calf god. When the two Torahs were harmonized it created several parallel statements and stories, often with different geographical locations.

To further complicate the geography, a third name was applied to it in the *Book of Judges*, which is considered by scholars to be the oldest surviving texts that have not been heavily redacted by later priesthoods. In Song of Deborah, found in *Judges*, the mountain where God came down to the Israelites is called Mount Seir, and the details of the story she repeats are the same as those of the Sinai event. Fortunately, this does narrow the list of possible mountains to the southern Abarim mountains in modern Jordan, south of the Dead Sea. In this verse, the author identified Horeb as being eleven days away from Mount Seir, which supports Horeb and Sinai being different locations, with Horeb being to the west of the Arabah, likely at Hashem El Tarif, near the modern Egyptian-Israeli border.

The 1st century Jewish General and Historian Josephus, who was given the ancient scrolls from the Second Temple when Rome destroyed it, claimed that ancient records indicated that Mount Sinai was in the Roman province of Arabia Petra, and was between Egypt and Arabia. This itself does little to clarify where it was, as Arabia Petra encompassed the entire Sinai Peninsula, as well as southern modern Israel, Jordan, and northwest Saudi Arabia, however, it does appear to have been an accurate report of what the ancient scrolls recorded as the disciple Paul reported the same thing. Paul was a Pharisee before his conversion to Christianity and quoted a lot of obscure Jewish texts in support of his ideology. Paul's claim that Sinai was in Arabia, is generally accepted as meaning the Roman province of Arabia Petra, as he was a Roman citizen, as does not appear to have ever left the empire. In order to simplify the reading of this translation, the southern Hor is called Hor, while the northern Hor is called Nur.

**10** Codex Vaticanus: Sēir (cɦɪꝑ)

• Septuagint manuscript 630: Sieir (cιⲇꝑ)

• Septuagint manuscript 318: Sēēr (cⲏⲏꝑ)

• Septuagint manuscript 108: Seieir (cⲇⲇꝑ)

• Septuagint manuscript 19: Seteir (cⲟτⲇꝑ)

• Septuagint manuscript 72: Siēr (cιⲏꝑ)

• Septuagint manuscript 106: Sēr (cⲏꝑ)

• Septuagint manuscript 618: Sēēir (cⲏⲏⲓꝑ)

• Dead Sea Scroll 4QDeut[h]: Šŏyr (שׂעיר)

• Leningrad Codex: Śē'îr (שֵׂעִיר)

• Shapira scrolls: -ŏyr (꒐ᴢ°-) in a later verse; this verse was not in the scroll. The scroll was damaged, however, likely read Šŏyr (꒐ᴢ°w) before being damaged.

• Peshitta: Sŏyr (ܣܥܝܪ)

• Targum Onkelos: Śē'îr (שֵׂעִיר)

• Targum Jerusalem: Gablā' (גַבְלָא)

• Targum Pseudo-Jonathan: Gablā' (גַבְלָא)

- Sahidic manuscript 296L: Seir (Ceip)
- Sahidic manuscript 2001: not mentioned in the verse
- Sahidic manuscript 2006: Sueir (Cyeip)
- Sahidic manuscript 2178L: Sēeir (CHeip)

Mount Seir was identified as being in Edom in *Cosmic Genesis*, where Abraham's son Esau's descendants lived. Mount Seir was not mentioned in *Exodus*, *Leviticus*, or *Numbers*, but was mentioned in the Song of Deborah, found in *Judges*, as the mountain where God came down to the Israelites, and the details of the story she repeats are the same as those of the Sinai Event, implying Seir was another name for Sinai. Seir was also mentioned in the Egyptian el-Amarna Letters, written between 1360 and 1332 BCE, were the Nomads (Shasu) of Sôr lived, somewhere in the Abarim mountains of modern southwest Jordan.

**11** Codex Vaticanus: Kadēs Barnē (ĸᴀᴅʜcʙᴀpɴʜ)

- Septuagint manuscript 319: Kaddēs Barnē (ĸᴀᴀᴧᴧc βapᴧ)
- Septuagint manuscript 669: Kaddēs Barnei (ĸᴀᴀᴧc βapᴎ)
- Septuagint manuscript 71: Kaddēs Barni (ĸᴀᴀᴧc βapᴎɪ)
- Septuagint manuscript 53: Kaddēs Barnōs (ĸᴀᴀᴧᴧc βapᴎooc)

- Dead Sea Scroll 4QDeut^h: Qdš Brnô (ברנו קדש). Translation: sacred Brnow (or Vrnow)

- Leningrad Codex: qādēš Barnēa' (קָדֵשׁ בַּרְנֵעַ). Translation: Sacred Barnea (or Varnea)

- Shapira scrolls: qdš brnô (ברנו קדש) in a later verse; this verse was not in the scroll.

- Peshitta: rqm dhyå (ܪܩܡ ܕܚܝܐ). Translation: various (or numbers of) life

# CHAPTER 1

- Targum Onkelos: rəqam gê'â (רְקַם גֵּיאָה). Translation: various (or numbers of) gorges (or ravines)
- Targum Jerusalem: rəqam dəgê'â' (רְקַם דְּגֵיעָא). Translation: numbers (or various) of gorges (or ravines)
- Targum Pseudo-Jonathan: rəqam gê'â (רְקַם גֵּיאָה). Translation: various (or numbers of) gorges (or ravines)
- Sahidic manuscript 296L: Kadēs Barnē (ⲔⲁⲆⲎⲤ ⲂⲁⲢⲚⲎ)
- Sahidic manuscript 2001: not mentioned in the verse

The location of Kadesh Barnea has been debated since the Second Temple Era. The Jewish general and historian Josephus reported that the sacred books salvaged from the Second Temple when it was destroyed by the Romans placed Kadesh Barnea at Petra, in modern Jordan. He also claimed that Mount Sinai was nearby, which is the source of the claim that Mountain of the Altar (Jebel al-Madhbah) was Mount Sinai. The name Kadesh Barnea is undoubtedly named after an ancient deity, as the first word, kadesh (קדש), means holy or sacred. The name Barnea, more commonly pronounced as Varne'a in Hebrew, is presumably the name of the deity in question, and is quite similar to the name Mitannian Indo-Aryan (Vedic) god Varuna. As *Deuteronomy* chapter 2 goes on to report that there were Hurrians living in Seir before the Edomites killed them and inhabited the region, this would support the name Varuna being the source of Barnea, as the Hurrians were the major population base of the Mitanni Empire. This connection between the Mitannian Indo-Aryan Varuna worshipers at Mount Seir would also explain how the name Mitra-Varuna (𒈪𒆠 𒀸𒇷) entered into Judaism, as his earliest recorded Hebrew name Mttrwn (מטטרון) is essentially the same as the Mitannian Miitra-Aruna, and played the same role in the Vedic Texts as Metatron did in Second Temple Era Judaism. Subsequent Hebrew pronunciations of the name from the Medieval Era, Mttrwn (מטטרון), Metātərôn (מְטָטְרוֹן), Mətatrôn

CHAPTER 1

(מְטַטְרוֹן), Mêtatrôn (מִיטַטְרוֹן), Mîtatrôn (מִיטַטְרוֹן), and Mattatrôn (מַטַטְרוֹן), as well as the Arabic Mītatrūn (ميططرون), are all influenced by the Greek pronunciation of the name Metà-thrónos (Μετὰ-θρόνος), which means "next to the throne."

**12** Papyrus Fouad 266 (LXX 847, 848 and 942): Yhwh (𐤉𐤄𐤅𐤄)

The dating of the Papyrus Fouad 266 is debated. It's likely a copy of an older text created after the 12th century. The text style suggests the original manuscript dates to between the 1st century BCE and the 1st century CE. It is a fragment of the Septuagint with the name Yhwh (יהוה) written in Hebrew or Aramaic in gaps that are the correct length to write Kurios (Κυριος). However, it also includes the subscript iota, invented in the 12th century. It might have been created for a Christian or Islamic museum, or simply as a hoax. It is unclear how much the later scribe deviated from the original manuscript, and the name may have been in the document since it was created. This would make it an early Kaige redaction.

• Codex Vaticanus: KS (κ̄ς̄). Translation: lord
• Leningrad Codex: Yəhwâ (יְהֹוָה)
• Peshitta: mryå (ܡܪܝܐ). Translation: master
• Targum Onkelos: Yəyā (יְיָ). Translation: Yahweh
• Targum Jerusalem: not mentioned in the verse
• Targum Pseudo-Jonathan: Yəyā (יְיָ). Translation: Yahweh

This verse does not survive intact in any fragments of the Dead Sea Scrolls or Shapira Scrolls, however, the name Yahweh is found in other verses that have survived.

• Dead Sea Scroll 1QDeutᵃ: Yhwh (𐤉𐤄𐤅𐤄)
• Dead Sea Scroll 1QDeutᵇ: Yhwh (𐤉𐤄𐤅𐤄)
• Dead Sea Scroll 4QDeutᵃ: Yhwh (𐤉𐤄𐤅𐤄)
• Dead Sea Scroll 4QDeutᵇ: Yhwh (𐤉𐤄𐤅𐤄)

- Dead Sea Scroll 4QDeut<sup>c</sup>: Yhwh (𐤉𐤄𐤅𐤄)
- Dead Sea Scroll 4QDeut<sup>d</sup>: Yhwh (𐤉𐤄𐤅𐤄)
- Dead Sea Scroll 4QDeut<sup>e</sup>: Yhwh (𐤉𐤄𐤅𐤄)
- Dead Sea Scroll 4QDeut<sup>f</sup>: Yhwh (𐤉𐤄𐤅𐤄)
- Dead Sea Scroll 4QDeut<sup>g</sup>: Yhwh (𐤉𐤅𐤄𐤉)
- Dead Sea Scroll 4QDeut<sup>h</sup>: Yhwh (𐤉𐤅𐤄𐤉)
- Dead Sea Scroll 4QDeut<sup>i</sup>: Yhwh (𐤉𐤄𐤅𐤄)
- Dead Sea Scroll 4QDeut<sup>j</sup>: Yhwh (𐤉𐤅𐤄𐤉)
- Dead Sea Scroll 4QDeut<sup>k1</sup>: Yhwh (𐤉𐤅𐤄𐤉)
- Dead Sea Scroll 4QDeut<sup>k2</sup>: Yhwh (𐤉𐤄𐤅𐤄)
- Dead Sea Scroll 4QDeut<sup>l</sup>: Yhwh (𐤉𐤄𐤅𐤄)
- Dead Sea Scroll 4QDeut<sup>m</sup>: Yhwh (𐤉𐤅𐤄𐤉)
- Dead Sea Scroll 4QDeut<sup>n</sup>: Yhwh (𐤉𐤅𐤄𐤉)
- Dead Sea Scroll 4QDeut<sup>o</sup>: Yhwh (𐤉𐤄𐤅𐤄)
- Dead Sea Scroll 4QDeut<sup>p</sup>: Yhwh (𐤉𐤄𐤅𐤄)
- Dead Sea Scroll 4QDeut<sup>q</sup>: Yhwh (𐤉𐤄𐤅𐤄)
- Dead Sea Scroll 4QpaleoDeut<sup>r</sup>: Yhwh (𐤉𐤄𐤅𐤄)
- Dead Sea Scroll 5QDeut: Yhwh (𐤉𐤄𐤅𐤄)
- Shapira scrolls: Yhwh (𐤉𐤄𐤅𐤄)
- Sahidic manuscript 296L: joeis (ϫoⲉⲓⲥ). Translation: master (or mistress)

The name Yahweh (יהוה) was transliterated as Iaō (Ιαω) in some books of the Septuagint, however, no early copies of *Deuteronomy* survive that include the name Iaō (Ιαω). The Papyrus Fouad 266 is a fragment of a copy of *Deuteronomy* in which the name Yhwh (יהוה) was placed into the Greek text in Aramaic or Hebrew script. Other documents like it are generally viewed as being Kaige redactions from the 1<sup>st</sup> or 2<sup>nd</sup> century CE. The situation of the

# CHAPTER 1

Fouad fragments is curious though. The paleography suggests the text was written in the 1$^{st}$ century BCE, however, includes the Iota subscript that was not invented until the 12$^{th}$ century. It is unclear why it was created.

The space in between the Greek words and the name is long enough to write Kurios (Κυριος), indicating that the original Greek scribe did not plan to write the name in the text. A second Aramaic or Hebrew scribe then added the name, however, the scribe that copied the manuscript did not move the words closer together. It may have been for an Islamic college or a Christian museum. The scribe was probably copying something ancient, however, knew the contemporary form of Greek, and added the subscripts iotas. This suggests the manuscript he worked from was already quite damaged, supporting the idea that it dated to the Classical era. Scholars debate the age of older the manuscript, largely placing it between the 1$^{st}$ century BCE and 2$^{nd}$ century CE. Other scholars reject this as proof of an ancient manuscript, and date it to after the 12$^{th}$ century.

The name Yhwh (𐤉𐤄𐤅𐤄 / יהוה) is in almost all fragments of *Deuteronomy* found among the Dead Sea Scrolls, however, almost all of these scrolls have been dated to the Hasmonean Dynasty or later, and most are in the Aramaic "block" script, the official script of the Hasmonean Dynasty. There are a few exceptions though, 4QpaleoDeut$^r$ is a fragment of *Deuteronomy* written in the Phoenician script that includes the name Yhwh (𐤉𐤄𐤅𐤄). 4QpaleoDeut$^r$ also dates to the Hasmonean Dynasty, and was therefore likely a copy written for the Samaritans, who continued using the old script. 4QDeut$^{k2}$ is an Aramaic script text from the later Herodian dynasty that uses the name Yhwh in the older Phoenician script, which indicates that by the Hasmonean Dynasty Judeans were accepting that the name was always in *Deuteronomy*. 5QDeut is the only fragment of *Deuteronomy* currently dated to

# CHAPTER 1

before the Hasmonean Dynasty that includes the name, however, is written in the Aramean script indicating it was likely written during the Maccabean Revolt that created the Hasmonean Dynasty. The dating of 1QDeut[a] and 1QDeut[b] also remain unclear, and may be earlier than the Romans Era (6 to 390 CE), however, as they are also in the Aramean script, are unlikely to date to earlier than the Hasmonean Dynasty.

**13** Codex Vaticanus: $\overline{KS}$ o $\overline{TS}$ ēmōn (ΚϹΟΘϹΗΜΩΝ). Translation: Lord the god of mine

• Septuagint manuscript 19: Kurios o teos o teos ēmōn (Κυβιος ο θεος ο θεος ἡμων). Translation: Lord the god the god of mine

• Septuagint manuscript 71: Kurios o teos ymōn (Κυβιος ο θεος υμων). Translation: Lord the god of y'all

• Dead Sea Scroll 1QDeutb: -h ålhy (אלהי ה-) survives. Translations: [Yahwe]h my god

• Dead Sea Scroll 4QDeut[h]: Yhwh ålhy (אלהי יהוה). Translation: Yahweh my god

• Leningrad Codex: Yəhwâ 'ĕlōhênû (יְהֹוָה אֱלֹהֵינוּ). Translation: Yahweh our god

This phrase survives in part or full, in multiple Dead Sea Scrolls, although in later verses as most do not have the beginning of *Deuteronomy* chapter 1.

• Peshitta: mryå ålhn (ܡܪܝܐ ܐܠܗܢ). Translation: master gods

• Targum Onkelos: Yyā 'ĕlāhānā' (יְיָ אֱלָהָנָא). Translation: Yahweh our god

• Targum Pseudo-Jonathan: Yyā 'ĕlāhên (יְיָ אֱלָהֵין). Translation: Yahweh gods

• Shapira scrolls: ålhm ålhnw (𐤀𐤋𐤄𐤌 𐤀𐤋𐤄𐤍𐤅). Translation: goddesses our goddess

43

# CHAPTER 1

• Sahidic manuscript 296L: pjoeis pennoute (ⲡϫⲟⲉⲓⲥ ⲡⲉⲛⲛⲟⲩⲧⲉ). Translation: the master (or mistress) of god (or divine)

• Sahidic manuscript 2001: not mentioned in the verse

The Aramaic sections of Masoretic Daniel that were not translated into Hebrew maintain the term 'ădōnāy hā'ĕlōhîm (אֲדֹנָי הָאֱלֹהִים), meaning the "lord of the gods" where the Septuagint has "Lord the god" (Κύριοσ ὁ θεὸσ). As most books of the Septuagint were translated from Aramaic texts, the Aramaic text almost certainly used the term 'ădōnāy hā'ĕlōhîm where the Septuagint has "Lord the god." The name Yahweh appears to have been added to most of the books in the Masoretic texts when they were translated to Hebrew during the Hasmonean Dynasty of Judea, between 140 and 37 BCE. According to the records from the time, this was to repair the damage King Manasseh had done 600 years earlier when he removed the name Yahweh from the Torah, however, no evidence has survived from the era of Manasseh or earlier that proves the name was originally in the text. This suggesting it was an attempt by the first Hasmonean High-Priest/King Simon the Zealot to create a national Judean religion with a god having a name similar to the Roman god Jove.

The name Yahweh, in the Aramaic form of Yhw (𐡉𐡄𐡅^) and Egypto-Aramaic form of Yāw (𐡉𐡀𐡅^), does appear to have originally been in some of the books of the Septuagint, such as *Leviticus*, which originated under the rule of King Josiah or later, and Yhw was a popular god among Judeans and Israelites under Persian and Greek rule. The translators at the Library of Alexandria transliterated this name as Iaō (Ιαω) in the books it was originally in, however, under the Hasmonean Dynasty it seems to have been added to all the books translated into Hebrew, creating some confusion among early Christians.

# CHAPTER 1

There were debates in the early Christian era about which version of the Israelite scriptures to use, the Greek, Hebrew, Samaritan, or Syriac translations, resulting in different versions of the scriptures being used by different churches. Some versions replaced the name Lord with Iaw in the Greek texts, either in the Greek form as Ιαω, or by copying in the Hebrew form of the name Yhwh (יהוה) or the older Phoenician form of Yhwh (𐤉𐤄𐤅𐤄), or by mocking the Hebrew with Greek letters as ΠΙΠΙ. This created a great deal of confusion among Christians, and ultimately the books of the Septuagint that had the name Iaw in them were redacted so all the books used the term Lord (Κύριοσ). Most Christian translations, as well as Jewish translations, have continued to use the term "Lord" in place of the name Yahweh, due to the prohibition on using any names of God that was introduced during the Hasmonean dynasty.

There are no early surviving copies of the Septuagint's version of *Deuteronomy* which have the name Iaō (Ιαω / 𐤉𐤄^) in them, like some of the other books of the Septuagint, and therefore it cannot be proven if the name was in the Septuagint's *Deuteronomy* or not, however, the terms used in Septuagint's *Deuteronomy* are consistent with the surviving Aramaic sections of Masoretic Daniel, strongly suggesting the Egypto-Aramaic source text the Greek translators used, included the term Adonai h'elahin, and not Yåw h'elahin. The Aramaic term meant "Lord of the gods," however, has been interpreted several ways within monotheistic religions, including the Jewish "powers of Yahweh" and Christian "Lord of the Trinity."

**14** Codex Vaticanus: Araba (ⲀⲢⲀⲃⲀ)

- Septuagint manuscript 246: Arouba (Ⲁⲣⲟⲩⲩⲁ)

- Septuagint manuscript 422: Arraba (Ⲁⲣⲣⲁⲩⲁ)

45

- Septuagint manuscript 120: Ara (ﺍﺭﺍ)

- Septuagint manuscript 767: Saraba (ﺳﺎﺭﺍﺑﺎ)

- Leningrad Codex: 'ărābâ (עֲרָבָה). Translation: plain

- Shapira scrolls: Órbh (ﻑﺝﻕﻩ)

- Peshitta: Órbå (ﺍﺭﺑﺎ)

- Targum Onkelos: mêšərayyā' (מֵישְׁרַיָּא). Translation: plain (or even, straight)

- Targum Pseudo-Jonathan: mêšərā' (מֵישְׁרָא). Translation: plain (or even, straight)

- Codex Lugdunensis (LV 100): Arabin (ARABIN)

- Sahidic manuscript 296L: Arba (ⲀⲢⲂⲀ)

- Sahidic manuscript 2001: Araba (ⲀⲢⲀⲂⲀ)

- Bohairic manuscripts: Areba (ⲀⲢⲉⲂⲀ)

Arabah was the name for the region south of the Dead Sea.


**15** Codex Vaticanus: uious gigantōn (ⲨⲒⲞⲨⲤ ⲄⲒⲄⲀⲚⲦⲰⲚ). Translation: sons of Gigantes (in ancient Greek, or giants in modern Greek)

- Septuagint manuscript 28: uios Gigantōn (ⲩⲟⲥ Γιγαντῶ). Translation: son of Gigantes

- Leningrad Codex: bənê 'Ănāqîm (בְּנֵי עֲנָקִים). Translation: sons of Anakites (or neck, necklace, or giant in modern Hebrew)

- Peshitta: bny gnbrå (ﺑﻨﻲ ﺟﻨﺑﺭﺍ). Translation: sons of heroes

- Targum Onkelos: bənê gibbārā'ê (בְּנֵי גִבְרָאֵי). Translation: sons of heroes

- Targum Pseudo-Jonathan: bənê 'eprôn gibbārā' hămênā' (בְּנֵי עֶפְרוֹן גִּבְרָא חֲמֵינָא). Translation: sons of Ephron hero of his kind

- Sahidic manuscript 296L: šere nnGigas (ϢⲎⲢⲉ ⲚⲚⲄⲒⲅⲀⲤ). Translation: child of the giants

# CHAPTER 1

The Anaks were transliterated as Enach (Εναχ) in *Numbers*, and Enacim (Ενακιμ) later in *Deuteronomy*, but translated as Gigantes in this verse, implying the Greeks considered the Anaks to be like the Gigantes of ancient Greece, who fought a war against the Olympian gods, and lost. The Anaks (Anakim) were a tribe of people also referred to in the books of *Joshua* and *Judges*. According to *Judges*, they apparently lived in Hebron. The Egyptian Execration Texts from the Middle Kingdom (circa 2050 to 1650 BCE) record a group of Canaanites called the "ly Anaq" who are generally considered to be the same people. The name Anaks is restored in this translation from the Leningrad Codex, as that does appear to be their name.

# CHAPTER 2

We turned and departed into the wilderness, by the way of the Sea of Edom, as the Lord told me, and we surrounded Mount Seir for many days.

The Lord said to me, "You have encompassed this mountain long enough, turn therefore toward the north. Order the people, "You are going through the borders of your brothers the children of Esau, who live in Seir, and they will fear you, and dread you greatly. Do not engage in war against them, for I will not give you their land even enough to set your foot on, for I have given mount Seir to the children of Esau as an inheritance. Buy food from them for silver and eat, and you will receive water from them by measure for silver, and drink."

Our lord of the gods has blessed you in every work of your hands. Consider how you traveled through that great and terrible wilderness. Look, the lord of the gods has been with you forty years, you did not lack anything. We passed by our brothers the children of Esau, who lived in Seir, by the way of Arabah from Aelon and from Eziongaber, and we turned and passed by the way of the desert of Moab.

The Lord said to me, "Do not you quarrel with the Moabites, and do not engage in war with them, for I will not give you of their land as an inheritance, for I have given Seir[1] to the children of Lot to inherit. Formerly the Emims lived in it, a great and numerous nation and powerful, like the Anaks. These also will be counted as Rephaim[2] like the Anaks[3] (who the Moabites call Emims).[4] The Hurrians[5] lived in Seir before, and the sons of Esau destroyed them, and completely consumed them from before them. They lived in their place, as Israel did in the land of his inheritance, which the Lord gave to them.

Now then I said, "Arise and depart, and cross the valley of Zered."

The days in which we traveled from Kadesh Barnea until we crossed the Valley of Zered, were thirty-eight years, until the whole generation of the men of war failed, dying out of the camp as the lord of the gods swore to them. The hand of the Lord was on them to destroy them out from among the camp until they were consumed. It came to pass when all the men of war died out from among the people, that the Lord spoke to me, saying, "Today you will pass over the borders of Moab to Aroer, and you will come close to the children of Amman.[6] Do not quarrel with them, or wage war against them, for I will not give you the land of the children of Amman as an inheritance, because I have given it to the children of Lot as an inheritance. It will be counted as a land of Raphain, for the Raphain lived there before, (the Ammonites call them Zamzums).[7] A great nation and populous, and mightier than you, like the Anaks, yet the Lord destroyed them out from before them, and they inherited their land, and they lived there instead of them until this day. As they did to the children of Esau that live in Seir, even as they destroyed the Hurrians from before them, and inherited their country, and lived there instead of them until this day."

"The Mitanni[8] who live between Azzah and Gaza,[9] and the Minoans[10] who came out of Crete,[11] destroyed them and lived in their space. Now then, arise and depart, and pass through the valley of Arnon. Look, I have delivered into your hands Sihon the king of Heshbon the Amorite, and his land. Begin to inherit it. Engage in war with him today. Begin to put your terror and your fear on the face of all the nations under the sky, who will be troubled when they have heard your name, and will be in anguish before you."

I sent ambassadors from the wilderness of Kedemoth to Sihon king of Heshbon with peaceable words, saying, "I will pass through your land. I will go by road. I will not turn aside to the right hand or to the left. You will sell me food for silver, and I will eat, and you will sell me water for silver, and I will drink. I will only go through on my feet, as the sons of Esau allowed me, who lived in Seir, and the Moabites who lived in Aroer, until I have crossed the Jordan into the land which our lord of the gods gives us."

Sihon king of Heshbon would not agree that we should pass by, because our lord of the gods hardened his spirit, and made his heart stubborn, that he might be delivered into your hands, as on this day. The Lord said to me, "Look, I have begun to deliver before you Sihon the king of Heshbon the Amorite, and his land, and begin to inherit his land. Sihon the king of Heshbon came out to meet us, he and all his people to war at Jahaz. Our lord of the gods delivered him before our

# CHAPTER 2

face, and we destroyed him, and his sons, and all his people. We took possession of all his cities at that time, and we completely destroyed every city in succession, and their wives, and their children. We left no living victims, except we took the livestock captive and took the spoil of the cities. From Aroer, which is by the brink of the Arnon River, and the city which is in the valley, and as far as Mount Gilead, there was not a city that escaped us. Our lord of the gods delivered all of them into our hands. Only we did not come close to the children of Amman, even all the parts bordering on the brook of Jabbok, and the cities in the mountain country, as our lord of the gods ordered us.

## CHAPTER 2 NOTES

**1** Codex Vaticanus: Sēeir (ⲥⲏⲉⲓⲣ)

• Septuagint manuscript 19: Aroēr (ⲁⲉⲟⲏⲣ)

• Septuagint manuscript 108: Arōēr (ⲁⲉⲱⲏⲣ)

• Septuagint manuscript 120: Aroeir (ⲁⲉⲟⲓⲣ)

• Septuagint manuscript 370: Aoēr (ⲁⲟⲏⲣ)

• Septuagint manuscript 53: Artēr (ⲁⲣⲑⲏⲣ)

• Septuagint manuscript 551: Aroēn (ⲁⲉⲟⲱ)

• Septuagint manuscript 106: Gar (ⲅⲁⲣ)

• Septuagint manuscript 799: Gēn (ⲅⲏⲱ)

• Septuagint manuscript 107: Siēr (ⲥⲓⲏⲣ)

• Septuagint manuscript 82: Siēir (ⲥⲓⲇⲣ)

- Septuagint manuscript 707: Asēr (ܐܣܝܪ)
- Septuagint manuscript 74: Asēir (ܐܣܝܪ)
- Septuagint manuscript 602: Asēēr (ܐܣܝܝܪ)
- Leningrad Codex: 'Ār (עָר)
- Shapira scrolls: Ôr (אֹ)
- Targum Onkelos: ləḥāyāt (לְחָיָת)
- Targum Pseudo-Jonathan: ləḥāyayt (לְחָיְיַת)
- Vetus Latina manuscript 100: Seir (Seir)
- Sahidic manuscripts 17: Sēeir (Cнeιp)

Moab was reported to be the son/grandson of Lot by his elder daughter, supporting the reading of "Seir" in this verse, however, Seir is already identified as being in the territory of the Edomites, suggesting the boundaries of Moab and Edom moved during the forty-year interlude. However, the Shapira scrolls supports the Hebrew reading of 'Ār. 'Ār is mentioned several times in *Numbers* and *Isaiah*, however, the name is not translated consistently between the languages, with Greek manuscripts including variants Sier and Ēr. Variations of Aroer are also used in the Old Armenian and Coptic translations, While the Vetus Latin manuscripts use Here.

No ruins have been linked to 'Ār, although those who believe it existed generally place it in the southern part of the Arnon Valley. The books of *Numbers* and *Judges* also seem to disagree on who lived in the region before King Sihon of the Amorites conquered it, with the *Numbers* reporting Moabites lived there, and *Judges* reporting the Ammonites lived there. As both Moab, the patriarch of the Moabites, and Ben-Ammi, the patriarch of the Ammonites, were reported to have been Lot's sons/grandsons by his daughters, it is plausible that the Ammonites were viewed as a Moabite tribe during the late Bronze Age, when the stories are set, and did not develop into unique nations until the Iron Age.

**2** Codex Vaticanus: Rafain (ΡΑΦΑΙΝ)

- Septuagint manuscript 509: Rafaeim (ΡΑϤΑϤμ)

- Septuagint manuscript 59: Rafaēn (ΡΑϤΑⲗⲱ)

- Leningrad Codex: Rəpā'îm (רְפָאִים). Translation: long-dead (or a tribe generally transliterated as Rephaites)

- Peshitta: gnbrå (ܓܢܒܪܐ). Translation: heroes (or giants)

- Targum Onkelos: gibbārā'ê (גִּבָּרָאֵי). Translation: heroes

- Targum Pseudo-Jonathan: gibbārayā' (גִּבָּרַיָּא). Translation: heroes (or giants)

- Bohairic manuscripts: Rafain (Ⲣⲁⲫⲁⲓⲛ)

- Shapira scrolls: Rpåm (𐤓𐤐𐤀𐤌)

- Sahidic manuscripts 2001: Rafaein (Ⲣⲁⲫⲁⲉⲓⲛ)

The Raphites (𐤓𐤐𐤀𐤌) were semi-deified by the 1200s BCE, as the Ugaritic texts include the so-called Rephaim Text. They appear to be an ancient people that had been deified and were believed to live in the underworld. The word's etymology implies they were healers.

**3** Codex Vaticanus: Enak (ⲈⲚⲀⲔ)

- Codex Freer Greek MS. V (LXX WI): Ainak (ⲀⲒⲚⲀⲔ)

- Septuagint manuscript 509: Ennak (Ⲉⲛⲛⲁⲕ)

- Septuagint manuscript 426: Enakim (Ⲉⲛⲁⲕⲓμ)

- Septuagint manuscript 72: Senak (Ⲥⲁⲛⲁⲕ)

- Leningrad Codex: 'Ănāqîm (עֲנָקִים). Translation: Anakites (or neck, necklace, or giant in modern Hebrew)

- Peshitta: gnbrå (ܓܢܒܪܐ). Translation: heroes (or giants)
- Targum Onkelos: gibbārā'ê (גִּבָּרָאֵי). Translation: heroes
- Targum Pseudo-Jonathan: ginbərayā' (גִנְבְּרַיָא)
- Codex Lugdunensis (VL 100): Senak (Sᴇɴᴀᴋ)
- Munich Palimpsest (VL 104): Aenac et unianimes sunt (Aᴇɴᴀᴄ ᴇᴛ ᴜɴɪᴀɴɪᴏ̨ᴇꜱ ꜱᴜɴᴛ). Translation: Aenac and they are unanimous
- Sahidic manuscript 2001: efjoor (ᴇϥxoop). Translation: strong bodies

**4** Codex Vaticanus: Ommin (oᴍᴍɪɴ)
- Codex Alexandrinus (LXX A): Oommein (ooᴍᴍᴇɪɴ)
- Codex Ambrosiano A 147 (LXX F): Emmein (ᴇᴍᴍᴇɪɴ)
- Septuagint manuscript 630: Omien (Oμḍν)
- Septuagint manuscript 318: Ommēn (Oμμⳑⲱ)
- Septuagint manuscript 426: Ommim (Oμμμ)
- Septuagint manuscript 125: Omin (Oμν)
- Septuagint manuscript 646: Ommiein (Oμμⳑν)
- Septuagint manuscript 537: Êmmein (Ḥμμⳑν)
- Septuagint manuscript 59: Omiēn (Oμⳑⲱ)
- Septuagint manuscript 376: Ommieim (Oμμⳑμ)
- Leningrad Codex: 'ēmîm (אֵמִים). Translation: terrors (or threateners, frighteners)
- Shapira scrolls: Åmm (𐤀𐤌𐤌)
- Peshitta: Åmnå (ܐܡܢܐ). Translation: task (or art, evil, carefreeness)
- Targum Onkelos: 'Êmətānê (אֵימְתָנֵי)
- Targum Pseudo-Jonathan: 'Êmətānê (אֵימְתָנֵי)

- Codex Lugdunensis (VL 100): Omitte (Oⲱⲓⲧⲧⲉ)
- Sahidic manuscript 17: Ommein (Oⲙⲙⲉⲓⲛ)
- Sahidic manuscript 2001: Ommiein (Oⲙⲙⲓⲉⲓⲛ)
- Sahidic manuscript 2006: Ommēneim (Oⲙⲙⲏⲛⲉⲓⲙ)

The scribal note suggests that the text was used in Moab, and the note was added for the Moabites. The book of *Deuteronomy* is sometimes interpreted as an anti-Moabite text that had been written to discredit the prophet Balaam and the gods of Moab. This note, and other Moabite translations in the book, indicate that there was an earlier version of the book before it was used in Moab.

**5** Codex Vaticanus: Ǩorrạion (ⲭⲟⲣⲣⲁⲓⲟⲛ)

- Septuagint manuscript 30: Ǩōrrạion (χωββₐ⁄ⲱ)
- Septuagint manuscript 46: Ǩoraion (χοβₐ⁄ⲱ)
- Septuagint manuscript 610: Amorrạion (ⲁμοββₐ⁄ⲱ)
- Septuagint manuscript 767: Ǩōraion (χωβₐ⁄ⲱ)
- Leningrad Codex: Hōrîm (חֹרִים). Translation: Hurrians
- Shapira scrolls: Hrm (𐤉𐤋𐤄)
- Peshitta: Hwryå (ܚܘܪܝܐ)
- Targum Onkelos: Hōrā'ê (חֹרָאֵי)
- Targum Pseudo-Jonathan: Gənûsayā' (גְנוּסָיָא)
- Sahidic manuscript 17: Ǩorraios (Ⲭⲟⲣⲣⲁⲓⲟⲥ)

These appear to be the people the Egyptians called the Ǩårw (𓈎𓄿𓂋𓅱), which are known as the Hurrians in modern history books. The Hurrians were an ancient people in the Middle East, native to Northern Iraq, Syria, and eastern Turkey before the Semitic and Persian tribes migrated into the region. While they appear to have become a slave race for centuries under the rule of the Old Babylonian and Old Assyrian kingdoms, they became the dominant ethnic group of the Mitanni Empire between 1600 and 1300 BCE, after being freed by the Indo-Aryan Mitanni people.

**6** Septuagint manuscript 963: umōn Amman (ΥΜΩΝ ΑΜΜΑΝ). Translation: sons of Amman

• Codex Vaticanus: umōn Ammōn (ΥΙΩΝ ΑΜΜΩΝ). Translation: sons of Ammon

• Septuagint manuscript 616: uiōn Ammō (ϒοον Αμμω). Translation: sons of Ammo

• Septuagint manuscript 59: uiōn Amōn (ϒοον Αμων). Translation: sons of Amon

• Septuagint manuscript 527: umōn Amban (υμων Αμμαν). Translation: sons of Amban

• Leningrad Codex: bənê 'Ammôn (בְּנֵי עַמּוֹן). Translation: sons of Ammon

• Shapira scrolls: Ȯmnm (𐤏𐤌𐤍𐤌). Translation: Ammonites

• Peshitta: bny Ȯmwn (ܒܢܝ ܥܡܘܢ). Translation: sons of Ammôn

• Targum Onkelos: bənê 'Ammôn (בְּנֵי עַמּוֹן)

• Targum Pseudo-Jonathan: bənê 'Ammôn (בְּנֵי עַמּוֹן)

• Codex Lugdunensis (VL 100): filiorum Ammon (ꝼ ILIORUM AꝏꝋON). Translation: son of Ammon

• Sahidic manuscript 17: šēre Amman (ϣΗΡЄ ΝΑΜΜΑΝ). Translation: children of Amman

Amman was one of the nations to the east of Israel and later Judah, in modern Jordan, around the modern capital, Amman, which is named after the ancient Kingdom. As Amman is the modern city's name, Amman is used in this translation.

# CHAPTER 2

**7** Septuagint manuscript 963: Zozomen (ⲍⲟⲍⲟⲙⲉⲛ)

- Codex Vaticanus : Zokomein (ⲍⲟⲝⲟⲙⲉⲓⲛ)
- Codex Ambrosiano A 147: Zommein (ⲍⲟⲙⲙⲉⲓⲛ)
- Codex Freer Greek MS. V (LXX W¹): Zozommein (ⲍⲟⲍⲟⲙⲙⲉⲓⲛ)
- Codex Venetus (LXX V): Nozommin (ⲛⲟⲍⲟⲙⲙⲓⲛ)
- Septuagint manuscript 407: Ommein (ⲟⲙⲙⲇⲛ)
- Septuagint manuscript 509: Zokammein (ⲍⲟⲭⲇⲙⲙⲇⲛ)
- Septuagint manuscript 55: Zozommin (ⲍⲟⲍⲟⲙⲙⲓⲛ)
- Septuagint manuscript 64: Zomzommin (ⲍⲟⲙⲍⲟⲙⲙⲓⲛ)
- Septuagint manuscript 730: Zamzommin (ⲍⲇⲙⲍⲟⲙⲙⲓⲛ)
- Septuagint manuscript 318: Oozzommēn (ⲟⲟⲍⲍⲟⲙⲙⲩⲗⲩ)
- Septuagint manuscript 16: Zomzomin (ⲍⲟⲙⲍⲟⲙⲓⲛ)
- Septuagint manuscript 58: Zomzomein (ⲍⲟⲙⲍⲟⲙⲇⲛ)
- Septuagint manuscript 121: Zoommein (ⲍⲟⲟⲙⲙⲇⲛ)
- Septuagint manuscript 134: Zonzimmin (ⲍⲱⲍⲓⲙⲙⲩⲛ)
- Septuagint manuscript 313: Zomzomfeim (ⲍⲟⲙⲍⲟⲙⲫⲇⲙ)
- Septuagint manuscript 343: Zōmzommin (ⲍⲟⲟⲙⲍⲟⲙⲙⲓⲛ)
- Septuagint manuscript 426: Zomzommim (ⲍⲟⲙⲍⲟⲙⲙⲩ)
- Septuagint manuscript 707: Zōmmein (ⲍⲟⲟⲙⲙⲇⲛ)
- Septuagint manuscript 125: Zonzomin (ⲍⲱⲍⲟⲙⲩⲛ)
- Septuagint manuscript 130: Zomzompei (ⲍⲟⲙⲍⲟⲙⲡⲇ)
- Septuagint manuscript 646: Zōmzombim (ⲍⲟⲟⲙⲍⲟⲙⲩⲇⲩ)
- Septuagint manuscript 71: Zommin (ⲍⲟⲙⲙⲓⲛ)
- Septuagint manuscript 767: Zozomein (ⲍⲟⲍⲟⲙⲇⲛ)

- Septuagint manuscript 107: Zonzommin (ᴢ⊕ᴢ₀μμⱳ)
- Septuagint manuscript 52: Zomzombeim (ᴢ₀μᴢ₀μμⴑμ)
- Septuagint manuscript 106: Konzommin (ᴋ⊕ᴢ₀μμⱳ)
- Septuagint manuscript 321: Zomzompi (ᴢ₀μᴢ₀μπι)
- Septuagint manuscript 527: Zēzomēn (ᴢᴛᴢ₀μⱳ)
- Septuagint manuscript 46: Zomfeim (ᴢ₀μϐ⳿μ)
- Septuagint manuscript 59: Zomzommēn (ᴢ₀μᴢ₀μμⱳ)
- Septuagint manuscript 68: Zomnein (ᴢ₀μⱳⴑⱳ)
- Leningrad Codex: Zamzūmmîm (זַמְזֻמִּים)
- Shapira scrolls: Ôzmzmm (𐤏𐤆𐤌𐤆𐤌𐤌)
- Peshitta: Zmzyn (ܙܡܙܝܢ)
- Targum Onkelos: Ḥūšbānê (חֻשְׁבָּנֵי)
- Targum Pseudo-Jonathan: Zêmətānê (זֵימְתָנֵי)
- Codex Lugdunensis (VL 100): Zozomin (ᴢ0ᴢ0ᴍⁱɴ)
- Sahidic manuscript 2001: Zozommein (Ⲍⲟⲍⲟⲙⲙⲉⲓⲛ)
- Sahidic manuscript 2006: Zozomein (Ⲍⲟⲍⲟⲙⲉⲓⲛ)

The scribal note suggests that the text was used in Moab, and the note was added for the Moabites. The book of *Deuteronomy* is sometimes interpreted as an anti-Moabite text that had been written to discredit the prophet Balaam and the gods of Moab. This note, and other Moabite translations in the book, indicate that there was an earlier version of the book before it was used in Moab.

**8** Codex Vaticanus: Euaioi (ⲉⲨⲀⲓⲟⲓ)
- Septuagint manuscript 106: Euai (Ⲉⲩⲁⳇ)
- Leningrad Codex: 'Awwîm (עַוִּים)
- Peshitta: Ôwyå (ܥܘܝܐ)

# CHAPTER 2

- Targum Onkelos: 'Awwā'ê (עַוָּאֵי)

- Targum Pseudo-Jonathan: šə'ār pəlêtat Kəna'ănā'ê ( שְׁאָר פְּלֵיטַת כְּנַעֲנָאֵי). Translation: escaped remnants of the Canaanites

- Codex Lugdunensis (VL 100): Ebeu (ⲈⲂⲈⲨ)

- Sahidic manuscript 2001: Euhaois (ⲈⲨϨⲀⲒⲞⲤ)

The Greek term Euaioi (Ευαιοι) is a variation of Euaîon (Ευαῖον), which is usually mirrored in the Hebrew translation with Hiwwî (חִוִּי), however, in *Deuteronomy* it mirrored by 'Awwîm (עַוִּים).

In the Hebrew translation, Hiwwî (חִוִּי) is used interchangeably with Hōrî (חֹרִי). Hōrî is accepted as referring to the Hurrians, which the Egyptians called Ǩårw (𓅱𓂝𓂋𓎛), and the Babylonians called Ǩuurri (𒄯𒊑). The Hurrians were one of the oldest cultures in the Middle East, however, became largely a slave culture within the Akkadian and Old Babylonian empires. Under the Mitanni empire, they rose to a position of wealth, and formed the noble caste. The Greek transliteration of this term was Ǩorŗaious (Χορραιους), which, like the Hebrew term, was used interchangeably in the texts with Euaîon (Ευαῖον) / Hiwwî (חִוִּי), although that term generally applied to the rules and priests.

The ultimate origin of the terms Euaîon (Ευαῖον), 'Awwîm (עַוִּים), and Hiwwî (חִוִּי), both appear to be the cuneiform word Éan (𒂍𒀭), meaning temple or sacred. In the Amarna Letters, which date to the 1330s BCE, the term Éan (𒂍𒀭) was the name of a people, who appear to be the Mitanni, or a group within the Mitanni. A similar correlation between the terms is found in the 1ˢᵗ Paralipomenon and Dibrê-hayyāmîm, where the Greek translation uses Baitani (Βαιθανι), however, the Hebrew uses the term Mitnî (מִתְנִי). This term also refers to a group of people, meaning the underlying Edomite text the Greeks translated would have been "people of the" House of Ån (𐤁𐤉𐤕𐤀𐤍), a direct Canaanite translation of É An (𒂍𒀭).

# CHAPTER 2

While Mitni was the transliteration used in the Edomite text that formed the basis of the Hebrew translation of Dibrê-hayyāmîm, it was replaced with Ḥiwwî (חִוִּי) in the Judahite texts, which served as the basis of most of the Masoretic texts. This likely originated in a Judahite copy of the text, after the Aramaic translation had been made, where an N (𐤉) was replaced with a W (𐤅). The Aramaic translation would have already been made in the time of King Manasseh, were the term was transliterated as Hyản (𐡇𐡉𐡍), itself a transliteration of the early Canaanite Ḥyản (𐤇𐤉𐤍). The term 'Awwîm (עַוִּים) found in *Deuteronomy*, which originated in Samaritan, appears to have maintained a closer transliteration of the cuneiform Éan (𒂍𒀭), based on the Neo-Sumerian pronunciation of Ayam.

**9** Septuagint manuscript 963: Asērōṯ eōs Gazēs (ⲀⲤⲎⲢⲰⲐ ⲈⲰⳞ ⲄⲀⲌⲎⳞ). Translation: Aseroth before Gaza

• Codex Vaticanus: Asēdōṯ eōs Gazēs (ⲀⲤⲎⲆⲰⲐ ⲈⲰⳞ ⲄⲀⲌⲎⳞ). Translation: Asedoth before Gaza

• Septuagint manuscript 52: Asirōṯ eōs Gazēs (Ⲁⲟⲓⲣⲱⲑ ⲟⲟⳞ ⲅⲁⲍⲏⳞ). Translation: Asiroth before Gaza

• Septuagint manuscript 120: Aseirōṯ eōs Gazeis (Ⲁⲟⲉⲓⲣⲱⲑ ⲟⲟⳞ ⲅⲁⲍⲓⳞ). Translation: Aseiroth before Gaza

• Septuagint manuscript 767: Pasērōṯ eōs Gazēs (ⲡⲁⲟⲏⲣⲱⲑ ⲟⲟⳞ ⲅⲁⲍⲏⳞ). Translation: Paseroth before Gaza

• Septuagint manuscript 527: Nasērrōṯ eōs Gazēs (Ⲛⲁⲟⲏⲣⲣⲱⲑ ⲟⲟⳞ ⲅⲁⲍⲏⳞ). Translation: Naserrhoth before Gaza

• Leningrad Codex: ḥăsērîm 'ad-'Azzâ (חֲצֵרִים עַד־עַזָּה). Translation: yards (or courtyards) to (or on, until) Gaza

# CHAPTER 2

• Peshitta: ḥsrym wôdmå lÔåzå (ܣܝܢ ܘܥܕܡܐ ܠܥܙܐ). Translation: yards (or courtyards) and until Gaza

• Targum Onkelos: dəpîaḥ 'ad 'Azzâ (דְּפִיחַ עַד עַזָּה). Translation: the soot until (or while) Gaza

• Targum Pseudo-Jonathan: Diprîa' 'ad 'Azzâ (דִּפְרִיעַ עַד עַזָּה). Translation: Dipria until (or while) Gaza

• Codex Lugdunensis (VL 100): Asaroth usque Gazan (Asaroth usque Cazan). Translation: Asaroth all the way to Gaza

• Sahidic manuscript 2001: Asērōt̠ šahrai eGaza (ⲁⲥⲏⲣⲱⲑ ϣⲁϩⲣⲁⲓ ⲉⲅⲁⲍⲁ). Translation: Aseroth unward (or down to) Gaza

**10** Codex Vaticanus: Kappadokes (ⲕⲁⲡⲡⲁⲇⲟⲕⲉⲥ). Translation: Cappadocians

• Septuagint manuscript 376: Kappodokes (Καπποδοκⲉ́ⲥ)

• Septuagint manuscript 646: Kappadokai (Καππⲁδοⲓⲁⲩ)

• Septuagint manuscript 46: Kappadokis (Καππⲁδοⲓⲇⲥ)

• Septuagint manuscript 619: Kappadokoi (Καππⲁδοⲕⲟⲓ)

• Septuagint manuscript 707: Kappadōkes (Καππⲁδⲟⲟⲓⲅ́ⲥ)

• Septuagint manuscript 767: Kampadokes (Καμπⲁδοⲓⲅ́ⲥ)

• Leningrad Codex: Kaptōrîm (כַּפְתֹּרִים). Translation: Caphtorites

• Peshitta: Qpwdqyå (ܩܦܘܕܩܝܐ)

• Targum Onkelos: Qappûtəqā'ê (קְפוֹטְקָאֵי)

• Targum Pseudo-Jonathan: šə'ār pəlêtat Kəna'ănā'ê (שְׁאָר פְּלֵיטַת כְּנַעֲנָאֵי). Translation: escaped remnants of the Canaanites

• Sahidic manuscript 2001: Kappadokos (ⲕⲁⲡⲡⲁⲇⲟⲕⲟⲥ). Translation: Cappadocians

This translation accepts the common translation of Caphtor as Crete, meaning the Caphtorites would have been the Minoans.

# CHAPTER 2

Archaeological and genetic evidence has proven that the Minoans traded and settled the coastal regions of the eastern Mediterranean between 2500 and 1500 BCE, including northern Egypt and ancient Canaan as far south as the Midian Mountains of northwest Saudi Arabia.

The Mandean messenger/angel Ptahil (ࡐࡕࡀࡄࡉࡋ) is generally viewed as being based on the Egyptian creator god Ptah (𓊪𓏏𓎛), whom the Egyptians claimed originated in Minoan Crete, suggesting the Kaftorim in Canaan may have referred to a cult, not the ethnic group themselves.

**11** Septuagint manuscript 963: Kappadokias (ΚΑΠΠΑΔΟΚΙΑϹ). Translation: Cappadocia

• Codex Ambrosiano A 147: Kapadokias (ΚΑΠΑΔΟΚΙΑϹ)

• Septuagint manuscript 707: Kapadōkias (ΚΑΠΑΔΩΚΙΑϹ)

• Septuagint manuscript 313: Kappodokias (ΚΑΠΠΟΔΟΚΙΑϹ)

• Septuagint manuscript 767: Kampadokias (ΚΑΜΠΑΔΟΚΙΑϹ)

• Septuagint manuscript 75: Kappadōkias (ΚΑΠΠΑΔΩΚΙΑϹ)

• Septuagint manuscript 53: -ppadokias (-ΠΠΑΔΟΚΙΑϹ)

• Leningrad Codex: Kaptôr (כַּפְתּוֹר). Translation: Caphtor (or Minoan Crete)

• Peshitta: Qpdwqy (ܩܦܕܘܩܝ)

• Targum Onkelos: Qappûtəqayyā' (קְפּוֹטְקְיָא)

• Targum Pseudo-Jonathan: Qappûtəqəyā'â (קְפּוֹטְקְיָאה)

• Sahidic manuscript 2001: Kappadokia (ΚΑΠΠΑΔΟΚΙΑ). Translation: Cappadocia

Caphtor was mentioned in several surviving ancient texts from the 2nd millennium BCE, including the Mari Tablets, dated to circa 1770 BCE, Thutmose III's Hymn of Victory, from circa 1450 BCE, and the Ras Sharma Texts from Ugarit, dated to circa 1340 BCE. *Cosmic Genesis / Bereshít* refers to Caphtor as a son of Mizraim (Egypt), which implies a colony of Egypt, while the Ras Sharma Texts uses the name Caphtor as the name of the home of the Canaanite god Kothar-wa-Khasis, which is accepted as the Canaanite version of the Egyptian god Ptah.

The location of Caphtor was already long lost and debated by the time the Septuagint was translated at the Library of Alexandria, which supports the antiquity of the *Book of Deuteronomy*. At the time, Greek translators believed it was in Cappadocia, in central modern Turkey, most likely associating it with the civilization today referred to as the Neshites (Hittites), however, the Egyptian records that mention Kftyw (𓎡𓆑𓏏𓇋𓅱), list it as being a port city, and Cappadocia was an inland nation. This identification of Caphtor with Cappadocia is based on its location in Thutmose III's biography, from circa 1450 BCE, which placed Caphtor as Thutmose's northernmost conquest, and his Empire had conquered all of Canaan, and extended to the border of Cappadocia.

Jewish scholars have traditionally rejected Cappadocia as the location of Caphtor. In the 1st century CE, the Judean historian and general Josephus wrote in his Antiquities of the Judeans, that the Caphtorites were an Egyptian people whose city was destroyed in a war with the Æthopians (presumably Kushites) and migrated to Philistia (the modern Gaza Strip). Other Jewish sources, such as Maimonides, in the 12th century CE, have placed Caphtor in the Nile Delta.

Early Christians accepted the Greek identification of Caphtor as Cappadocia, and Cappadocia was the translation of Caphtor that Jerome chose for the Vulgate in the 4th century. Modern scholars have debated the issue, with many locations suggested, including Cicilia (southern Turkey), Cyprus, Crete, or some other island in the Aegean Sea.

# CHAPTER 2

Currently, the academic view is that either Cicilia or Crete are the most likely locations of Caphtor, however, the archaeological evidence from Crete shows that some major force burnt almost every town in Crete during the life of Thutmose III, which his biography claims he did to Caphtor, and therefore, the terms Crete and Cretan are used in this translation.

# CHAPTER 3

We turned and went by the path leading to Bashan, and Og[1] the king of Bashan came out to meet us, he and all his people, to battle at Edrei. The Lord said to me, "Don't fear him, for I have delivered him and his people and land, into your hands, and you will do to him as you did to Sihon king of the Amorites who lived in Heshbon."

Our lord of the gods delivered him into our hands, even Og the king of Bashan, and all his people, and we destroyed him until we left none of his seed. We conquered all his cities at that time, there was not a city which we did not take from the. Sixty cities and all the country around Lajat, belonging to king Og in Bashan: all of which were strong cities, with high walls, gates, and bars. As well as many cities of the Perizzites. We completely destroyed them as we dealt with Sihon the king of Heshbon, so we completely destroyed every city in order, and the women and the children, and all the livestock, and we took as conquest for ourselves the spoil of the cities. At that time we took the land out of the hands of the two kings of the Amorites, who were beyond the Jordan, extending from the Arnon[2] River all the way to Hermon.[3] (The Phoenicians[4] call Hermon Sanior,[5] and the Amorites called it Shenir.)[6]

All the cities of Misor,[7] and all Gilead,[8] and all Bashan[9] as far as Salkhad[10] and Daraa,[11] cities of the kingdom of Og in Bashan. For only Og the king of Bashan was left of the Raphain. His bed was a bed of iron, it is in the citadel city of the children of

Ammon, the length of it is nine cubits, and the width of it four cubits, according to the cubit of a man. We inherited that land at that time from the ruins[12] that are by the border of the Arnon River, and half the hills of Gilead. I gave his cities to Reuben and to Gad. The rest of Gilead, and all Bashan the kingdom of Og I gave to the half-tribe of Manasseh, and all the country around Lajat,[13] all of Bashan, it will be counted as the land of Raphain. Jair the son of Manasseh took all the country around Lajat as far as the borders of Geshuri and Maachathi: he called them by his name Bashan Thavoth Jair until this day.

To Machir I gave Gilead. To Reuben and to Gad I gave the land under Gilead as far as the Arnon River, the border between the river and as far as Jabbok, the river is the border to the children Amman. Arabah and Jordan are the boundaries of the Sea of Galilee[14] and east of the Sea of Arabah (the Sea of Salt),[15] past Asedoth east of the Phasga.[16] I ordered you at that time, "The lord of the gods has given you this land by lot. Arm yourselves, everyone that is powerful, and go before your brothers the children of Israel. Only your wives and your children and your livestock (I know that you have much livestock), let them remain in the cities which I have given you. Until the lord of the gods gives your brothers rest, as also has he given to you, and they also will inherit the land, which our lord of the gods gives them on the other side of Jordan. then you will return, each one to his inheritance which I have given you."

I commanded Joshua at that time, "Your eyes have seen all things, which our lord of the gods did to these two kings, so will our lord of the gods will do to all the kingdoms against which you meet over there. You will not be afraid of them, because our lord of the gods himself will fight for you."

I implored the Lord at that time, "Lord of the gods, you have begun to show to your servant your strength, and your power, and your mighty hand, and your high arm: for what god is there in the sky or on the earth, who will do as you have done, and according to your might? I will, therefore, go over and see this good land that is beyond Jordan, this good mountain and Anti-lebanon. Because of you, the Lord did not regard me or listened not to me."

The Lord replied to me," Let it be enough for you, don't speak of this matter to me anymore. Go up to the top of the quarried rock, and look with your eyes westward, and northward, and southward, and eastward, and look at it with your eyes, for you will not go over this Jordan. Order Joshua, and strengthen him, and encourage him, as he will go before the face of these people, and he will give them the inheritance of all the land which you have seen."

We lived in the valley near the house of Peor.

## CHAPTER 3 NOTES

**1** Septuagint manuscript 963: Ōg (ܘܓ)

- Codex Vaticanus: Gōg (ܓܘܓ)

- Septuagint manuscript 767: Nōg (Νωγ)

- Leningrad Codex: 'Ôg (עוֹג)

# CHAPTER 3

- Shapira scrolls: Ôg (𐤏𐤂)
- Peshitta: Åwg (ܐܘܓ)
- Targum Onkelos: 'Ôg (עֹוג)
- Targum Pseudo-Jonathan: 'Ôg (עוֹג)
- Sahidic manuscript 2001: Ōg (ⲱⲅ)


**2**  Codex Vaticanus: Arnōn (ΑΡΝⲰΝ)
- Leningrad Codex: 'Arnōn (אַרְנֹן)
- Shapira scrolls: Årnn (𐤀𐤓𐤍𐤍)
- Peshitta: Årnwn (ܐܪܢܘܢ)
- Targum Onkelos: 'Arnōn (אַרְנֹן)
- Targum Pseudo-Jonathan: 'Arnônā' (אַרְנוֹנָא)
- Sahidic manuscript 2001: Arnōn (ⲁⲣⲛⲱⲛ)

Generally identified as Wadi Mujib in Jordan, a river canyon that flows into the Dead Sea.


**3**  Septuagint manuscript 963: Aermōn (ΑⲉⲣⲘⲰⲚ)
- Codex Ambrosiano A 147: orous Aermōn (ⲟⲣⲟⲩⲥⲁⲉⲣⲙⲱⲛ). Translation: Mount Hermon
- Codex Colberto-Sarravianus: orous Ermōn (ⲟⲣⲟⲩⲥⲉⲣⲙⲱⲛ). Translation: Mount Hermon
- Leningrad Codex: har Ḥermôn (הַר חֶרְמֹון). Translation: Mount Hermon
- Peshitta: twrå dHrmwn (ܛܘܪܐ ܕܚܪܡܘܢ). Translation: mount of Hermon
- Targum Onkelos: ṭûrā' dəHermôn (טוּרָא דְחֶרְמֹון). Translation: mount of Hermon
- Targum Pseudo-Jonathan: ṭawwrā' dəHermôn (טַוְורָא דְחֶרְמֹון). Translation: mount of Hermon

# CHAPTER 3

• Sahidic manuscript 2001: šahrai eaErmōn (ϣⲁϩⲣⲁⲓ ⲉⲁⲉⲣⲙⲱⲛ). Translation: upper of Ermon

• Sahidic manuscript 2006: šahrai eaErnōn (ϣⲁϩⲣⲁⲓ ⲉⲁⲉⲣⲛⲱⲛ). Translation: upper of Ernon

Mount Hermon is still known, as the southernmost major peak in the Anti-Lebanon mountain range, on the border of Syria, Lebanon, and the Israeli-occupied Golan Heights. The peak is currently occupied by a UN Peace Keeping Force.

**4** Codex Vaticanus: Foinikes (ⲫⲟⲓⲛⲓⲕⲉⲥ). Translation: Phoenicians

• Septuagint manuscript 75: Finikes (Φινικϭϲ)

• Septuagint manuscript 318: Funikes (Φυνικϭϲ)

• Leningrad Codex: Sîdōnîm (צִידֹנִים). Translation: Sidonians

• Peshitta: Sydnyå (ܨܝܕܢܝܐ). Translation: Sidonians

• Targum Onkelos: Sîdōnā'ê (צִידֹנָאֵי)

• Targum Jerusalem: Sîdônā'ê (צִידוֹנָאֵי)

• Targum Pseudo-Jonathan: Sîdônā'ê (צִידוֹנָאֵי)

• Sahidic manuscript 2006: Foinix (ⲫⲟⲓⲛⲓⲝ). Translation: Phoenicians

The Sidonians were a Canaanite people from the city of Sidon. Phoenician was the Greek name for the Canaanites.

**5** Septuagint manuscript 920: Saniōr (ⲥⲁⲛⲓⲱⲣ)

• Codex Freer Greek MS. V: Saneiōr (ⲥⲁⲛⲉⲓⲱⲣ)

• Septuagint manuscript 422: Sanēōr (Cⲇⲫⲗⲱⲟⲃ)

• Septuagint manuscript 75: Sanaōr (Cⲇⲫⲗⲟⲟⲃ)

• Septuagint manuscript 59: Aniōr (Ⲁⲛⲓⲟⲟⲃ)

# CHAPTER 3

- Septuagint manuscript 767: Sanriōn (ϲⲁⲛⲣⲓⲟⲟⲛ)

- Septuagint manuscript 53: Saniōn (ϲⲁⲛⲓⲟⲟⲛ)

- Septuagint manuscript 53: Sariōn (ϲⲁⲣⲓⲟⲟⲛ)

- Leningrad Codex: Śiryōn (שִׂרְיֹן)

- Peshitta: Srywn (ܣܪܝܘܢ)

- Targum Onkelos: Siryōn (סִרְיֹן)

- Targum Jerusalem: 'ar'ā' masrê pêrôhî (אַרְעָא מַסְרֵי פֵּירוֹהִי).
Translation: land of mouth-watering (or fruit producing) sin

- Targum Pseudo-Jonathan: tawwrā' dəmasrê pêrôy (טַוְורָא דְמַסְרֵי
פֵּירוֹי). Translation: mountain of sinful fruit

- Codex Lugdunensis (VL 100): Seir (Sⲉⲓⲣ)

- Sahidic manuscript 2001: Saniōr (ϲⲁⲛⲓⲱⲣ)

**6** Septuagint manuscript 920: Saneir (ϲⲁⲛⲉⲓⲣ)

- Septuagint manuscript 963: Aneir (ⲁⲛⲉⲓⲣ)

- Codex Venetus: Sanieir (ϲⲁⲛⲓⲉⲓⲣ)

- Septuagint manuscript 407: Saniēr (ϲⲁⲛⲓⲏⲣ)

- Septuagint manuscript 46: Sanir (ϲⲁⲛⲓⲣ)

- Septuagint manuscript 15: Sanēr (ϲⲁⲛⲏⲣ)

- Septuagint manuscript 392: Samir (ϲⲁⲙⲓⲣ)

- Septuagint manuscript 319: Sanior (ϲⲁⲛⲓⲟⲣ)

- Septuagint manuscript 458: Anir (ⲁⲛⲓⲣ)

- Septuagint manuscript 59: Aniēr (ⲁⲛⲓⲏⲣ)

- Leningrad Codex: Śənîr (שְׂנִיר)

- Peshitta: Snyr (ܣܢܝܪ)

- Targum Onkelos: Tûr Talgā' (טוּר תַּלְגָּא). Translation: Mount
Snow

- Targum Jerusalem: 'ar'ā' marbê pêrê 'îlānā' ( אַרְעָא מַרְבֵּי פֵּירֵי אִילָנָא). Translation: land of best fruit trees
- Targum Pseudo-Jonathan: Tawāwr Talgā' (טַוְור תַּלְגָא). Translation: Mount Snow
  - Codex Lugdunensis: Sanis (Sᴀɴɪꜱ)
  - Sahidic manuscript 2001: Saneir (Cᴀɴeɪp)
  - Sahidic manuscript 2044: Sanir (Cᴀɴɪp)
  - Bohairic manuscripts: Saniōur (Cᴀɴɪⲱⲧp)

**7** Septuagint manuscript 963: Meisōr (Meɪcⲱp)
- Codex Vaticanus: Misōr (Mɪcⲱp)
- Septuagint manuscript 707: Mēsōr (Mʜ Ⲥⲱⲣ)
- Septuagint manuscript 59: Miōr (Mɪooⲣ)
- Leningrad Codex: mîšōr (מִישׁוֹר). Translation: plain (or level country, table land)
- Peshitta: pqõtå (ܦܩܥܬܐ). Translation: plain (or level country, table land)
- Targum Onkelos: mêšərā' (מֵישְׁרָא). Translation: plains (or valleys, lowlands)
- Targum Pseudo-Jonathan: mêšərā' (מֵישְׁרָא). Translation: plains (or valleys, lowlands)
  - Codex Lugdunensis: Mysorum (Ⲙ̄ysoꞃⲩⲙ̄)
  - Sahidic manuscript 2044: Misōr (Mɪcⲱp)
  - Bohairic manuscripts: Nisōur (Nɪcⲱyp)

Misôr was also the name of a Canaanite god. The Greeks interpreted it as a land named after Misôr, while the Hebrew translation can simply be read as "table land."

**8** Codex Vaticanus: Galaad (ᴦᴀᴧᴧᴀᴧ)

- Septuagint manuscript 509: Balaan (ᴃᴧᴧᴧⲫ)
- Leningrad Codex: Gil'ād (גִּלְעָד)
- Peshitta: Glôd (ܓܠܥܕ)
- Targum Onkelos: Gil'ād (גִּלְעָד)
- Targum Pseudo-Jonathan: Gil'ād (גִּלְעָד)
- Codex Lugdunensis: Galatia (ᴄᴀʟᴀᴛⲓᴀ)
- Sahidic manuscript 2044: Galaad (ᴦᴀᴧᴧᴀᴧ)

Gilead was land now located in the Irbid, Ajloun, Jerash and Balqa Governorates of northwest Jordan. Galatia, the translation used in Vetus Latina manuscripts, was an unrelated land in central Anatolia, suggesting the early Latin translator did not know the geography of the region.

**9** Septuagint manuscript 920: Basan (ᴃᴀᴄᴀɴ)

- Septuagint manuscript 30: Bassan (ᴃᴧⲟⲟⲫ)
- Septuagint manuscript 121: Basa (ᴃᴧⲒⲁ)
- Leningrad Codex: Bāšān (בָּשָׁן)
- Shapira scrolls: Bšn (𐤁𐤔𐤍)
- Peshitta: Mtnyn (ܡܬܢܝܢ). Translation: Mitanni
- Targum Onkelos: Matnān (מַתְנָן)
- Targum Pseudo-Jonathan: Matnān (מַתְנָן)
- Codex Lugdunensis: Chasan (ᴄʜᴀꜱᴀɴ)
- Sahidic manuscript 2001: Basan (ᴃᴀᴄᴀɴ)

Bashan was the name off the rocky land located in modern southern Syria and the Golan Heights. The Aramaic Targums and Peshitta use the alternate term Mitanni, which does refer to the nation ruling the region in the bronze age, however, it is unclear where the name entered into the Aramaic translations, as it is not

# CHAPTER 3

found in the Hebrew, Greek, Coptic, or Latin translations. The term was forgotten by the beginning of the iron age, and not rediscovered until the 1800s, suggesting it may have been used in an older Samaritan version of *Deuteronomy*, and replaced at some point by Bashan, as Aramaic developed after the term had been forgotten.

**10** Septuagint manuscript 920: Elǩa (ⲉⲗ̄ⲭⲁ)

• Septuagint manuscript 407: Elǩan (Ⲉⲗⲭⲁ̀ⲩ)

• Septuagint manuscript 58: Selka (cⲑ̄ⲕⲁ)

• Septuagint manuscript 72: Elka (Ⲉⲗⲕⲁ)

• Septuagint manuscript 73: Laǩa (ⲗⲁⲭⲁ̌)

• Septuagint manuscript 120: Melǩa (ⲙ̄ⲑ̄ⲭⲁ̀)

• Septuagint manuscript 730: Selǩa (cⲑ̄ⲭⲁ̀)

• Leningrad Codex: Salkâ (סַלְכָה)

• Shapira scrolls: Ślkh (𐤔𐤋𐤊)

• Peshitta: Slkå (ܣܠܟܐ)

• Targum Onkelos: Salkâ (סַלְכָה)

• Targum Pseudo-Jonathan: Salwāwqî' (סְלְוֹוקְיא). Translation: Seleucia

• Codex Lugdunensis: Chelchat (Ⲥⲏⲉⲗⲥⲏⲁⲧ)

• Sahidic manuscript 2001: Selǩa (Ⲥⲉⲗⲭⲁ)

• Sahidic manuscript 2006: Sella (Ⲥⲉⲗⲗⲁ)

Salkhad is city in southern Syria, and the capital of Salkhad district, in as-Suwayda Governorate. The Targum Pseudo-Jonathan's substitution of Seleucia (סְלְוֹוקְיא) is strange as the targum is in Palestinian-Aramaic, meaning it originated in Palestine, and nearby Salkhad has never been abandoned. Selucia was the capital of

the Selucid Greek empire, between 305 and 240 BCE, suggesting
the substitution happened during the era, however, it is not found
in the Fragment Targums, which are in Judean-Aramaic and share
a lot of otherwise unique material with the Targum Pseudo-
Jonathan.

**11** Codex Vaticanus: Edraeim (ЄⲆⲢⲀЄⲒⲘ)

- Septuagint manuscript 64: Edrain (ЄⲆⲢⲀⲒⲚ)

- Septuagint manuscript 59: Edraēn (ЄⲆⲢⲀⲰⲚ)

- Septuagint manuscript 767: Aidraein (ⲀⲒⲆⲢⲀⲒⲚ)

- Septuagint manuscript 376: Edran (ЄⲆⲢⲀⲚ)

- Septuagint manuscript 707: Edraei (ЄⲆⲢⲀⲒ)

- Septuagint manuscript 82: Edra (ЄⲆⲢⲀ)

- Septuagint manuscript 71: Esdrain (ЄⲤⲆⲢⲀⲒⲚ)

- Septuagint manuscript 56: Esdraein (ЄⲤⲆⲢⲀⲒⲚ)

- Septuagint manuscript 53: Esdraeim (ЄⲤⲆⲢⲀⲒⲘ)

- Septuagint manuscript 319: Eudraein (ЄⲨⲆⲢⲀⲒⲚ)

- Septuagint manuscript 58: Esdraei (ЄⲤⲆⲢⲀⲒ)

- Leningrad Codex: 'Edre'î (אֶדְרֶעִי)

- Shapira scrolls: Ådróy (𐤀𐤃𐤓𐤏𐤉)

- Peshitta: Årdóy (ܐܪܕܥܝ)

- Targum Onkelos: 'Edre'î (אֶדְרֶעִי)

- Targum Pseudo-Jonathan: 'Edre'āt (אֶדְרֶעָת)

- Codex Lugdunensis: Chebrain (CⲎЄBRAⲒⲚ)

- Sahidic manuscript 2006: Edraein (ЄⲆⲢⲀЄⲒⲚ)

Edraeim/'Edre'î is the ancient name for Daraa, a city in southern
Syria, and the capital of Daraa district, and Daraa Governorate.

**12** Septuagint manuscript 920: Aroēr (ⲀⲢⲞⲎⲢ)

- Septuagint manuscript 58: Arōēr (ⲀⲉⲱⲎⲢ)

- Septuagint manuscript 30: Aroeir (ⲀⲉⲟⲓⲢ)

- Septuagint manuscript 46: Aroēn (Ⲁⲉⲟⲓⲱ)

- Septuagint manuscript 314: Roēr (ⲢⲟⲎⲢ)

- Septuagint manuscript 527: Asēr (ⲀⲥⲎⲢ)

- Leningrad Codex: 'ărō'ēr (עֲרֹעֵר). Translation: ruins

- Shapira scrolls: ôrôr (𐤅𐤁𐤅𐤁) in a different verse. Translation: ruins

- Peshitta: Årnwn (ܥܪܝܢ)

- Targum Onkelos: 'Ărō'ēr (עֲרֹעֵר)

- Targum Pseudo-Jonathan: 'Ărô'ēr (עֲרוֹעֵר)

- Sahidic manuscript 2001: Aroēr (ⲀⲢⲞⲎⲢ)

- Sahidic manuscript 2044: Naroēr (ⲚⲀⲢⲞⲎⲢ)

This is generally accepted as a reference to ancient ruins on the shore of the Arnon River, now known as the Wadi Mujib in Jordan. In chapter 2 Aroer was described as being on the banks of the Arnon, which would explain why the names are used interchangeably.

**13** Codex Vaticanus: Argob (ⲀⲢⲄⲞⲂ)

- Septuagint manuscript 407: Argōb (Ⲁⲃⲅⲟⲟⲩ)

- Septuagint manuscript 53: Argō (Ⲁⲃⲅⲟⲟ)

- Septuagint manuscript 318: Argōm (Ⲁⲃⲅⲟⲟⲙ)

- Septuagint manuscript 699: Arbok (Ⲁⲃⲩⲟⲓ)

- Septuagint manuscript 610: Argē (Ⲁⲃⲅⲏ)

- Septuagint manuscript 527: Araarbok (Ⲁⲉⲁⲟⲣⲩⲟⲓ)

- Leningrad Codex: 'Argōb (אַרְגֹּב)

# CHAPTER 3

- Shapira scrolls: Årgb (𐤀𐤓𐤂𐤁)
- Peshitta: Årgwb (ܐܪܓܘܒ)
- Targum Onkelos: Tərākônā' (טְרָכוֹנָא)
- Targum Jerusalem: 'Aṭarkûnā' (אַטַרְכוּנָא)
- Targum Pseudo-Jonathan: Targônā' (טַרְגוֹנָא)
- Sahidic manuscript 2001: Arbok (Ⲁⲣⲃⲟⲕ)
- Bohairic manuscripts: Arkôub (Ⲁⲣⲕⲱⲧⲃ)

Argob was an ancient name for the Lajat lava field in southern Syria, on the border of the Daraa and as-Suwayda Governorates.

**14** Septuagint manuscripts 920: Maǩanaraṯ (ⲘⲀⲬⲀⲚⲀⲢⲀⲐ)

- Codex Vaticanus: Maǩanareṯ (ⲘⲀⲬⲀⲚⲀⲢⲈⲐ)
- Codex Alexandrinus: Maǩenereṯ (ⲘⲀⲬⲈⲚⲈⲢⲈⲐ)
- Codex Freer Greek MS. V: Maǩanarad (ⲘⲀⲬⲀⲚⲀⲢⲀⲆ)
- Codex Venetus: Ǩeneret (ⲬⲈⲚⲈⲢⲈⲐ)
- Septuagint manuscript 407: Maǩaneret (ⲘⲀⲬⲁⲛⲣⲉⲑ)
- Septuagint manuscript 527: Maǩanarat (ⲘⲀⲬⲁⲛⲁⲣⲁⲧ)
- Septuagint manuscript 619: Maǩanatar (ⲘⲀⲬⲁⲛⲁⲧⲁⲣ)
- Septuagint manuscript 76: Manaraṯ (Ⲙⲁⲛⲁⲣⲁⲑ)
- Septuagint manuscript 75: Maǩandrad (ⲘⲀⲬⲁⲛⲇⲣⲁⲇ)
- Septuagint manuscript 458: Maǩandrad (ⲘⲀⲬⲁⲛⲣⲁⲇ)
- Septuagint manuscript 54: Maǩandrad (ⲘⲀⲬⲁⲇⲣⲁⲇ)
- Septuagint manuscript 376: Ǩanaraṯ (Ⲭⲁⲛⲁⲣⲁⲑ)
- Septuagint manuscript 68: Maǩaneret (ⲘⲀⲬⲁⲛⲣⲉⲑ)
- Septuagint manuscript 83: Maǩaeneret (ⲘⲀⲬⲁⲓⲛⲣⲉⲑ)
- Septuagint manuscript 59: Maǩenet (ⲘⲀⲬⲁⲩⲑ)
- Septuagint manuscript 30: Maǩanarad (ⲘⲀⲬⲁⲛⲁⲣⲁⲇ)

78

# CHAPTER 3

- Septuagint manuscript 85: Maǩenered (ΜΑχαρόΔ)
- Septuagint manuscript 73: Maǩenerd (ΜΑχαρΔ)
- Septuagint manuscript 16: Ǩenered (χαρόΔ)
- Septuagint manuscript 53: Ǩaneret̲ (χΔνρόθ)
- Septuagint manuscript 72: Ǩanet̲ (χΔνόθ)
- Leningrad Codex: mikKinneret (מִכִּנֶּרֶת). Translation: the Kinneret
  - Peshitta: mn Knrt (ܡܢ ܟܢܪܬ). Translation: the Kinneret
  - Targum Onkelos: migGēnôsar (מִגֵּנוֹסַר)
  - Targum Jerusalem: min Ginôsar (מִן גֵּנוֹסַר)
  - Targum Pseudo-Jonathan: miGnîsar (מִגְנִיסַר)
  - Codex Lugdunensis: Malechanaret (ⲘALECⲎANARET)
  - Sahidic manuscript 2001: Maǩanarat̲ (ⲘAⲬANAPAⲐ)

Kinneret is an alternate name for the Sea of Galilee, also known as Lake Tiberius.

**15** Septuagint manuscript 963: t̲alassēs Araba t̲alassēs alukēs (ⲐAⲖAⲤⲤⲎⲤ APABA ⲐAⲖAⲤⲤⲎⲤ AⲖYⲔⲎⲤ). Translation: Sea of Araba sea of salt

- Codex Ambrosiano A 147: t̲alassēs tou araba t̲alassēs alukēs (θΔλΔσσⲏc του ΔρΔuΔ θΔλΔσσⲏc Δλulⲏc). Translation: Sea of the Araba sea of salt
- Septuagint manuscript 44: t̲alassēs Araba t̲alassēs halukēs (θΔλΔσσⲏc APₑauΔ θΔλΔσσⲏc Δλulⲏc). Translation: Sea of Arraba sea of salt
- Septuagint manuscript 46: t̲alassēs Ara t̲alassēs halukēs (θΔλΔσσⲏc APₑα θΔλΔσσⲏc Δλulⲏc). Translation: Sea of Ara sea of salt

# CHAPTER 3

- Septuagint manuscript 71: eska kai Araba eôs talassēs halukēs (ⲥⲟⲭⲁ ⲗⲁⲓ ⲁⲉⲅⲁⲩⲁ ⲥ̄ⲟⲟⲥ ⲑⲁⲗⲁⲥⲟ̄ⲗⲥ ⲁⲗⲩⲗⲏⲥ). Translation: slit and Arabah from the sea of salt

- Septuagint manuscript 707: talassēs Raba talassēs halukēs (ⲑⲁⲗⲁⲥⲟ̄ⲗⲥ ⲣⲁⲩⲁ ⲑⲁⲗⲁⲥⲟ̄ⲗⲥ ⲁⲗⲩⲗⲏⲥ). Translation: Sea of Raba sea of salt

- Septuagint manuscript 767: talassēs Saraba talassēs halukēs (ⲑⲁⲗⲁⲥⲟ̄ⲗⲥ ⲥⲁⲣⲁⲩⲁ ⲑⲁⲗⲁⲥⲟ̄ⲗⲥ ⲁⲗⲩⲗⲏⲥ). Translation: Sea of Saraba sea of salt

- Leningrad Codex: yām hā'ărābâ yām hammelah (יָ֣ם הָעֲרָבָה֩ יָ֨ם הַמֶּ֜לַח). Translation: sea the plain sea the salt

- Peshitta: ymâ dÔrbâ ymâ dmlhâ (ܝܡܐ ܕܥܪܒܐ ܝܡܐ ܕܡܠܚܐ). Translation: sea of Arabah sea of salt

- Targum Onkelos: yammā' dəmêšərā' yammā' dəmilhā' (יַמָּא דְמֵישְׁרָא יַמָא דְמִלְחָא). Translation: sea of the plain sea of salt

- Targum Jerusalem: yamā' dəmêšərā' yamā' dəmilhā' (יַמָּא דְמֵישְׁרָא יַמָא דְמִלְחָא). Translation: sea of the plain sea of salt

- Targum Pseudo-Jonathan: yammā' dəmêšərā' (יַמָא דְמֵשְׁרָא). Translation: sea of salt

- Sahidic manuscript 2001: tetalassa nAraba tetalassa mmlh (ⲧⲉⲑⲁⲗⲁⲥⲥⲁ ⲛⲁⲣⲁⲃⲁ ⲧⲉⲑⲁⲗⲁⲥⲥⲁ ⲙⲙⲗⲁϩ). Translation: the sea of Araba the sea of salt

The Sea of Arabah was an ancient name for the Dead Sea. The fact that both the Greek and Hebrew translations include the same scribal note indicating that the Sea of Arabah was the Sea of Salt indicates that the Aramaic translator did not believe the term Sea of Arabah was commonly understood when the Aramaic translation was made.

This indicates that the translation was either made outside of Judea, or by immigrants, as the book of Ezra claims the Samaritan population was by the late Persian Era. It also indicates that the book must have been translated from an older version, presumably in Phoenician (Samaritan, Judahite, Ammonite, Moabite or Edomite) which used the older name.

**16** Septuagint manuscript 963: apo Asēdōt tēn Fasga anatolōn (ΑΠΟ ΑϹΗΔѠΘ ΤΗΝ ΦΑϹΓΑ ΑΝΑΤΟΛѠΝ). Translation: under (or past, near) Asedoth the Fasga eastward

• Codex Ambrosiano A 147: upo tēs Asēdōt tēn Faraŋga anatolōn (υπο τɧϲ ΔσɧΔοοθ τɧN ϕΔβΔγγΔ ΔNΔτολοοN). Translation: under (or past, near) the Asedoth the Faranga eastward

• Codex Venetus: apo Sēdōt tēn Faraŋga anatolōn (Δπο σɧΔοοθ τɧN ϕΔβΔγγΔ ΔNΔτολοοN). Translation: under (or past, near) Sedoth the Faranga eastward

• Septuagint manuscript 422: apo Asidōn tēn Fasgat anatolōn (Δπο ΔσιΔοοN ϯ ϕΔσγαθ ΔNΔτολοοN). Translation: under (or past, near) Asidon the Faranga eastward

• Septuagint manuscript 53: upo Asidōt tēn Faraŋga anatolōn (υπο ΔσιΔοοθ ϯ ϕαρΔγγα ΔNΔτολοοN). Translation: under (or past, near) Asidoth the Faranga eastward

• Septuagint manuscript 392: upo Asidōo tēn Fasga anatolōn (υπο ΔσιΔοοο ϯ ϕΔσγα ΔNΔτολοοN). Translation: under (or past, near) Asidōo the Fasga eastward

• Septuagint manuscript 72: upo Asidōd tēn Fasga anatolōn (υπο ΔσιΔοοΔ ϯ ϕΔσγα ΔNΔτολοοN). Translation: under (or past, near) Asidod the Fasga eastward

• Septuagint manuscript 767: upo Asidōn tēn Faga anatolōn (υπο ΔσιΔοοN ϯ ϕΔγα ΔNΔτολοοN). Translation: under (or past, near) Asidon the Faga eastward

# CHAPTER 3

- Septuagint manuscript 319: upo Asidōn tēn Fasgad anatolōn (υπο Ασιδων τῇ Φασγαδ ἀνατολῶν). Translation: under (or past, near) Asidon the Fasgad eastward

- Septuagint manuscript 59: upo Asēdōth tēn Farangan anatolōn (υπο Ασηδωθ τῇ Φαραγγαν ἀνατολῶν). Translation: under (or past, near) Asedoth the Farangan eastward

- Leningrad Codex: taḥat 'ašdōt happisgâ mizrāḥâ (תַּחַת אַשְׁדֹ֫ת הַפִּסְגָּה מִזְרָחָה). Translation: beneath the peak (or summit)the peak eastern

- Peshitta: dtḥyt Åšdwd wpsgå dbrmtå mn mdnḥå (דהׁחית אׁשדוד ܘܦܣܓܐ ܕܒܪܡܬܐ ܡܢ ܡܕܢܚܐ). Translation: beneath Ashdod and peak of bar-mata (meaning "outside native land" in Aramaic) in the east (or of sunshine)

- Targum Onkelos: təḥôt mašpak mərāmātā' madînəhā' (תְּחוֹת מַשְׁפַּךְ מְרָמָתָא מַדִינְחָא). Translation: beneath the ravines of the peak of the province

- Targum Jerusalem: təḥôt bêt šəpîkôt qîtəmā' min maddînəhā' (תְּחוֹת בֵּית שְׁפִיכוֹת קִיטְמָא מִן מַדִינְחָא). Translation: beneath the house of pouring of powder from the province

- Targum Pseudo-Jonathan: təḥôt šapkût mayā' mēramātā' maddînəhā' (תְּחוֹת שַׁפְכוּת מַיָּא מֵרַמְתָא מַדִינְחָא). Translation: beneath the pouring of house of the deceiver of the east

- Sahidic manuscript 2001: jin asēdōṯ peia nmma nša (ϫⲓⲛ ⲁⲥⲏⲇⲱⲑ ⲡⲉⲓⲁ ⲛⲙⲙⲁ ⲛϣⲁ). Translation: from Asedot valley of the rising sun

- Sahidic manuscript 2006: jin asētōṯ peia nmma nša (ϫⲓⲛ ⲁⲥⲏⲧⲱⲑ ⲡⲉⲓⲁ ⲛⲙⲙⲁ ⲛϣⲁ). Translation: from Asetot valley of the rising sun

# CHAPTER 4

Now Israel, hear the ordinances and judgments, all that I teach you today to do: that you may live, and be multiplied, and that you may go in and inherit the land, which the lord of the gods of your fathers gives you. You will not add to the word which I command you, and you will not take from it. Keep the commandments of our lord of the gods, all that I command you this day. Your eyes have seen all that our lord of the gods did in the case of Ba'al Peor, for every man that went to Ba'al Peor, the lord of the gods has completely destroyed him from among you. But you who kept close to the lord of the gods are all alive today.

Look, I have shown you ordinances and judgments as the Lord commanded me, that you should do so in the land into which you go to inherit. You will keep and do them, for this is your wisdom and understanding before all nations, as many as will hear all these ordinances, and they will say, "Look, this great nation is a wise and understanding people." For what manner of nation is so great, and which has a god so near to them as our lord of the gods is in all things in whatever we may ask of him? What manner of nation is so great, which has righteous ordinances and judgments according to all this law, which I set before you this day? Pay attention to yourself, and keep your mind diligent. Don't forget any of the things, which your eyes have seen, and don't let them depart from your heart all the days of your life.

# CHAPTER 4

You will teach your sons and your sons' sons, all the things that happened in the day in which you stood before our lord of the gods in Horeb in the day of the assembly, for the Lord said to me, "Gather the people to me, and let them hear my words, that they may learn to fear me all the days which they live on the earth,[1] and they will teach their sons."

You came close and stood under the mountain, and the mountain burned with fire up to the sky. There was darkness, blackness, and lightning. The Lord spoke to you out of the middle of the fire a voice of words, which you heard: and you saw nothing like it, you only heard a voice. He announced to you his covenant, which he commanded you to keep, including the ten commandments, and he wrote them on two tablets of stone. The Lord commanded me at that time, to teach you ordinances and judgments, that you should do them in the land which you go to inherit. Pay close attention to your hearts, as you saw no vision in the day in which the Lord spoke to you in Horeb in the mountain out of the middle of the fire. If you transgress and make for yourselves a carved image, any kind of figure, the figure of male or female, the figure of any animal that is on the earth, the figure of any winged bird which flies under the sky, the figure of any reptile which creeps on the earth, the figure of any fish of those which are in the waters under the earth, and in case having looked up to the sky, and having seen the sun and the moon and the stars, and all the order of the sky, you should go astray and worship them, and serve them, who the lord of the gods has distributed to all the nations under the sky. But God took you, and led you out of the land of Egypt, out of the iron furnace of Egypt, to be for him a people of inheritance, as you become today.

The lord of the gods was angry with me for the things you said and swore that I should not cross the Jordan and that I should not enter into the land, which the lord of the gods gives you for an inheritance. I die in this land, and will not cross over the Jordan, but you are to cross over and will inherit this good land. Pay attention to yourselves, in case you forget the covenant of our lord of the gods, which he made with you, and you transgress and make for yourselves a carved image of any of the things concerning which the lord of the gods commanded you. For the lord of the gods is a consuming fire, a jealous god. When you have fathered sons, and have grandsons, and you have lived a long time in the land, and have transgressed, and made a carved image of anything, and have done wickedly before the lord of the gods to provoke him, I call the sky and earth this day to witness against you, that you will certainly die-off from the land, into which you go across the Jordan to inherit. You will not prolong your days on it but will be completely cut off.

The Lord will scatter you among all nations, and you will be left few in number among all the nations, among which the Lord will bring you. You will serve other gods there, the works of the hands of men, wood and stones, which shall not see, nor can they hear, nor eat, nor smell. There you will seek the lord of the gods, and you will find him whenever you will seek him with all your heart, and with all your mind in your affliction. All these things will come on you in the last days, and you will return to the lord of the gods and will listen to his voice. Because the lord of the gods is a god of pity, he will not forsake you, nor destroy you. He will not forget the covenant of your fathers, which the Lord swore to them.

Ask about the former days which were before you, from the day when God created man on the earth, and beginning at the one end of the sky to the other end of the sky, if there has happened anything like this great event if such a thing has been heard when a nation has heard the voice of the living God speaking out of the middle of the fire, as you have heard and have lived. If God has decided to go and take for himself a nation out of the middle of another nation with trials and with signs, and with wonders, and with war, and with a mighty hand, and with a high arm, and with great sights, according to all the things which our lord of the gods did in Egypt in your sight. So that you should know that the lord of the gods is god, and there is none beside him. His voice was made audible from the sky to instruct you, and he showed you on the earth his great fire, and you heard his words out of the middle of the fire.

Because he loved your fathers, he also chose you as their seed after them, and he brought you with his great strength out of Egypt, to destroy nations greater and stronger than you in front of you, to bring you in, to give you their land to inherit, as you have it this day. You will know this day, and will consider in your heart, that the lord of the gods is god in the sky above, and on the earth beneath, and there is no one else but him. Keep his commandments, and his ordinances, all

# CHAPTER 4

that I command you this day, that it may go well with you, and with your sons after you, that you may be long-lived on the land, which the lord of the gods gives you forever.

Then Moses separated three cities beyond Jordan in the east, that the slayer might flee there, who should have slain his neighbor unintentionally, who he did not hate previously, and he will flee to one of these cities and live: Bosor in the wilderness, in the plain country of Reuben, and Ramoth in Gilead belonging to the Gadites, and Gaulon in Bashan belonging to Manasseh. This is the law that Moses set before the children of Israel. These are the testimonies, and the ordinances, and the judgments, which Moses spoke to the sons of Israel, when they came out of the land of Egypt, on the east side of Jordan, in the valley near the house of Peor, in the land of Sihon king of the Amorites, who lived in Heshbon, whom Moses and the sons of Israel destroyed when they came out of the land of Egypt. They inherited his land, and the land of Og king of Bashan, two kings of the Amorites, who were to the east of Jordant. From Aroer, which is on the border of the Arnon River, even to Mount Sihon, which is Hermon. All Arabah east of Jordan under Azzah, quarried in the rock.

## CHAPTER 4 NOTES

1 Codex Vaticanus: gēs (ΓΗϹ). Translation: land (or soil, Ge)

• Leningrad Codex: 'ădāmâ (אֲדָמָ֔ה). Translation: land (or Adamah)

• Targum Onkelos: 'ar'ā' (אַרְעָא). Translation: land (or ground)

- Targum Pseudo-Jonathan: 'ar'ā' (אַרְעָא). Translation: land (or ground)
  - Shapira scrolls: ådmh (𐤀𐤃𐤌𐤄). Translation: land (or Adamah)
  - Sahidic manuscript 2001: kah (ⲕⲁϩ). Translation: land (or district)

In the Canaanite religion, Adamah was the name of the goddess of the underworld, married to Resheph, the god of disease and healing. In the Hebrew version of the Torah, it is used as the name of the ground, or possibly the planet in the modern sense. In some Aramaic literature, Adamah was a fully-fledged goddess who could make her own decisions, however, she was still a personification of the ground, not an anthropomorphized goddess such as the Greek Rhea. The closest Greek counterpart would be Ge, who was also never anthropomorphized, although Adamah also had the role of underworld goddess, like Persephone, or the Mesopotamian Ereshkigal. Strangely, given the story of Korah's rebellion being tied to this location, and Adamah eating him, the earlier Greek name of Persephone was Korē (Κόρη).

# CHAPTER 5

Moses called all of Israel, and said to them, "Listen, Israel, to the ordinances and judgments, everything that I speak in your ears this day, and you will learn them, and observe and do them. The lord of the gods made a covenant with you in Horeb. The Lord did not make this covenant with your fathers, but with you: you are all here alive this day. The Lord spoke to you face to face in the mountain out of the middle of the fire. I stood between the Lord and you at that time to report to you the words of the Lord, (because you were afraid before the fire, and you did not go up to the mountain) saying, "I am the lord of the gods, who brought you out of the land of Egypt, out of the house of slavery. You will have no other gods before my face. You will not make for yourself an image, nor likeness of anything in the sky above, or whatever is in the earth beneath, and whatever is in the waters under the earth. You will not bow down to them, nor will you serve them; for I am the lord of the gods, a jealous god, visiting the sins of the fathers on the children to the third and fourth generation to those who hate me, and doing mercifully to thousands of them that love me, and that keep my commandments."

"You will not take the name of the lord of the gods in vain, for the lord of the gods will certainly not acquit him that takes his name in vain. Keep the sabbath day to sanctify it, as the lord of the gods commanded you. Six days you will work, and you will do all your works, but on the seventh day is the sabbath of the lord of the gods. You will do in it no work, you, nor your son, or your daughter, your man-slave or your woman-slave, your ox or your donkey, or all your livestock, or the foreigner who lives among you. Your man-slave may rest, and your woman-slave, and your ox, as well as you."

Remember that you were a slave in the land of Egypt, and the lord of the gods brought you out there with a mighty hand, and a high arm: therefore the Lord appointed you to keep the sabbath day and to sanctify it. Honor your father and your mother, as the lord of the gods commanded you. that it may be well with you, and that you may live long on the land, which the the lord of the gods gives you. You will not commit murder. You will not commit adultery. You will not steal. You will not bear false witness against your neighbor. You will not covet your neighbor's wife; you will not covet your neighbor's house, nor his field, nor his man-slave, nor his maid, nor his ox, nor his donkey, nor any animal of his, nor anything that is your neighbor's.

The Lord spoke these words to all the assembly of you, in the mountain out of the middle of the fire, there was darkness, blackness, storm, a loud voice, and he added no more, and he wrote them on two tablets of stone, and he gave them to me. It came to pass when you heard the voice out of the middle of the fire, for the mountain burned with fire, that you came to me, even all the heads of your tribes, and your elders, and you said, "Look, our lord of the gods has shown us his glory, and we have heard his voice out of the middle of the fire: this day we have seen that God will speak to man, and he will live. Now let us not die, for this great fire will consume us, if we will hear the voice of our lord of the gods anymore, and we will die. For what flesh is there which has heard the voice of the living God, speaking out of the middle of the fire, as we have heard, and will live? You go close and hear all that our lord of the gods will say, and you will tell us all things whatever our lord of the gods will tell you, and we will hear and obey."

The Lord heard the voice of your words as you spoke to me, and the Lord said to me, "I have heard the voice of the words of these people, even all things that they have said to you. They have said well all that they have spoken. If only there was such a heart in them, that they should fear me and keep my commands always, that it might be well with them and with their sons forever. Go, say to them, 'Return to your houses,' but stand here with me, and I will tell you all the commands, and the ordinances, and the judgments, which you will teach them, and let them do so in the land which I give them for an inheritance.

You will pay attention and do as the lord of the gods commanded you. You will not turn aside to the right hand or the left, from all the ways which the lord of the gods commanded you to walk in, that he may give you peace, and that it may be well with you, and you may prolong your days on the land which you will inherit.

# CHAPTER 6

These are the commands, and the ordinances, and the judgments, as many as Lord our god gave commandment to do in the land on which you enter to inherit it. That you will fear the lord of the gods, keep you all his ordinances, and his commandments, which I command you today, you, and your sons, and your grandsons, all the days of your life, that you may live many days. Therefore, listen Israel, and observe them, that it may be well with you, and that you may be greatly multiplied, as the lord of the gods of your fathers said that he would give you a land flowing with milk and honey.

These are the ordinances, and the judgments, which the Lord commanded the children of Israel in the wilderness when they had gone out from the land of Egypt. "Listen Israel, our lord of the gods is one the Lord. You will love the lord of the gods with all your mind, and with all your mind, and all your strength. These words, all that I command you this day, will be in your heart and your mind. You will teach them to your children, and you will speak of them sitting in the house, and walking by the way, and lying down, and rising. You will fasten them for a sign on your hand, and it will be immovable before your eyes. You will write them on the lintels of your houses and of your gates. It will come to pass when the lord of the gods has brought you into the land which he swore to your fathers, to Abraham, and Isaac, and to Jacob, to give you great and beautiful cities which you did not build, houses full of all good things which you did not fill, pools dug in the rock which you did not dig, vineyards and olive-yards which you did not plant, then having eaten and been filled, beware in case you forget that it was the lord of the gods that brought you out of the land of Egypt, out of the house of slavery."

"You will fear the lord of the gods, and him only will you serve. You will cling to him, and by his name, you will swear. Don't follow other gods of the nations around you, as the lord of the gods among you is a jealous god, in case the lord of the gods becomes very angry with you, and destroys you from off the face of the earth. You will not tempt the lord of the gods, as you tempted him in the temptation. You will, by all means, keep the commands of the lord of the gods, the testimonies, and the ordinances, which he commanded you. You will do that which is pleasing and good before the lord of the gods, that it may be well with you, and that you may go in and inherit the good land, which the Lord swore to your fathers, to chase all your enemies from in front of you, as the Lord foretold."

"It will come to pass when your son will ask you tomorrow, 'What are the testimonies, and the ordinances, and the judgments, which our lord of the gods has commanded us?'

Then you will answer your son, "We were slaves to Pharaoh in the land of Egypt, and the Lord brought us out there with a mighty hand, and with a high arm. The Lord gave signs and great and evil wonders in Egypt, Pharaoh, and his house in front of us. He brought us out there to give us this land, which he swore to give to our fathers. The Lord ordered us to observe all these ordinances, to fear our lord of the gods, that it may be well with us forever, that we may live, as even today. There will be mercy for us if we pay attention to keep all these commands before our lord of the gods, as he has commanded us."

# CHAPTER 7

When the lord of the gods brings you into the land which you go to possess, he will remove great nations from before you, the Cypriots,[1] Girgashites, Amorites, Canaanites, Perizzites, Mitannians, and Jebusites, seven nations more numerous and stronger than you, and the lord of the gods will deliver them into your hands, then you will destroy them. You will completely destroy them. You will not make a peace treaty with them, neither will you feel compassion for them, neither will you agree to marry them. You will not give your daughter to his son, and you will not take his daughter for your son. For he will draw away your son from me, and he will serve other gods. The Lord will be very angry with you, and will soon completely destroy you. You will do this to them: you will destroy their altars, and will break down their columns, and will cut down their groves, and will burn with fire the carved images of their gods.

You are a sacred people to the lord of the gods, and the lord of the gods chose you to be for him a unique people beyond all nations that are on the face of the earth. It was not because you are more numerous than all other nations that the Lord preferred you. The Lord chose you, as you are fewer in number than all other nations. Because the Lord loved you, and in keeping the oath which he swore to your fathers, the Lord brought you out with a strong hand, and the Lord redeemed you from the house of slavery, out of the hand of

# CHAPTER 7

Pharaoh king of Egypt. You will know, therefore, that the lord of the gods is god, a faithful god, who keeps covenant and mercy for them that love him, and for those that keep his commandments to a thousand generations, and who recompenses them that hate him to their face, to destroy them completely. Will not be relaxed with those that hate him: he will repay them to their face.

You will, therefore, obey the commands, and the ordinances, and the judgments, which I command you to do today. It will happen that when you have heard these ordinances, and have kept and done them, that the lord of the gods will keep the covenant and the mercy with you, which he swore to your fathers. He will love you, and bless you, and multiply you, and he will bless the offspring of your belly, and the fruit of your land, your grain, and your wine, and your oil, the herds of your oxen, and the flocks of your sheep, on the land which the Lord swore to your fathers to give to you. You will be blessed beyond all nations. There will not be among you an impotent or barren one, or among your livestock. The lord of the gods will remove from you all sickness, and none of the evil diseases of Egypt, which you have seen, and all that you have known, will he infect you with. He will infect them on all that hate you.

You will eat all the spoils of the nations which the lord of the gods gives you, your eye will not spare them, and you will not serve their gods for this is an offense for you. But if you should say in your heart, "This nation is greater than I, how will I be able to destroy them completely?" You will not fear them, you will certainly remember all that the lord of the gods did to Pharaoh and all the Egyptians: the great temptations which your eyes have seen, those signs and great wonders, the strong hand, and the high arm, how the lord of the gods brought you out. Likewise, the lord of the gods will do to all the nations, who you fear in their presence. The lord of the gods will send against them the hornets until they that are left and they that are hidden from you be completely destroyed. You will not be wounded by them, because the lord of the gods is among you, is a great and powerful god. The lord of the gods will consume these nations before you by little and little.

You will not be able to consume them quickly, in case the land becomes desert, and the wild beasts of the field are multiplied against you. The lord of the gods will deliver them into your hands, and you will destroy them with great destruction until you have completely destroyed them. He will deliver their kings into your hands, and you will destroy their name from that place. None will stand in opposition before you until you have completely destroyed them. You will burn with fire the carved images of their gods. You will not covet their silver, neither will you take for yourself gold from them, in case you should offend, because it is an abomination to the lord of the gods. You will not bring an abomination into your house, or you should be an accursed thing like it. You will completely hate it, and altogether despise it, because it is a cursed thing.

# CHAPTER 7

# CHAPTER 7 NOTES

**1** Septuagint manuscript 963: Ǩettaion (ⲭⲉⲧⲧⲁⲓⲟⲛ)

- Septuagint manuscript 46: Ǩetaion (ⲭⲉⲧⲁⲓⲱ)

- Leningrad Codex: Hittî (חִתִּי). Translation: Cypriots

- Peshitta: Hytyå (ܚܬܝܐ)

- Targum Onkelos: Hittā'ê (חִתָּאֵי)

- Targum Pseudo-Jonathan: Hittā'ê (חִתָּאֵי)

- Sahidic manuscript 17: Ǩettaios (ⲭⲉⲧⲧⲁⲓⲟⲥ)

This term has created a great deal of confusion since the misidentification of the ruins of the Neshites as being "Hittite" in the 1800s. The modern archaeological name "Hittite," is not derived from an ancient name for the culture applied by themselves, or anyone else, but rather adopted from the biblical reference to a then-unknown civilization somewhere in the region. There was an ancient culture in the region called the Hattians, however, they were conquered by the Nesites before 1700 BCE, and subsequently disappeared from the historic records.

The name was applied to culture today referred to as "Hittites," before the "Hittite" language had been translated, and is incorrect. Since 1906, excavations at Boğazköy, the ancient "Hittite" capital Hattusa have uncovered more than 10,000 "Hittite" texts, including the royal achieve. The actual name of the "Hittite" language and people was Nešili (𒀭𒉌𒅆), which is now rendered in some academic literate as Nesite or Neshite. As early as the mid-1800s some scholars disputed the identification of the Nesites as the Biblical Hittites, including the Orientalist Max Müller, who was one of many claiming the Biblical Hittites were ancient Greeks or some other Mediterranean people. Later in the Septuagint's translation of the Maccabees, the similar term Ǩettiim (Χεττιιμ) as a reference to all Greek-speaking lands, and therefore the Biblical Hittites were likely the Minoans or the Achaean Greeks.

In the 1st century CE, the Jewish historian Josephus reported that Ketima (Κετιμα) was the name of Cyrus in Aramaic, and the Kettiim were the descendants of Noah's grandson Ketimus, who had settled on Cyprus. Josephus reported that the name was preserved in the Greek name of the town Kition (Κίτιον). Most historians view it as more likely that the Aramaic name was derived from the city-state of Kition, which was known as Kåtjåy (𓈙𓂝𓐍𓇋𓅆) in Egyptian records from the New Kingdom Era in the late Bronze Age, and Kt (𐤕𐤊) or Kty (𐤉𐤕𐤊) in Phoenician records from the early Iron Age. While this may be the origin of the term, by the era of the Neo-Assyrian era, the term must have also referred to other Greek islands, as both the prophets Isaiah and Ezekiel used the term "Islands of Kittim."

As the term referred to the entire island of Cyprus in Aramaic, the translations of "Cyprus" and "Cypriots" are used here.

# CHAPTER 8

You will observe all the commands which I order you today, that you may live and be multiplied, and enter in and inherit the land, which the lord of the gods swore to give to your fathers. You will remember all the ways that the lord of the gods led you in the wilderness, when he punished you, and tried you, to test your in your heart whether you would keep his commandments or not. He punished you and straightened you with hunger, and fed you with manna, which your fathers did not know to teach you that man does not live by bread alone, but by every word that proceeds out of the mouth of God does man live. Your garments did not grow old and fall from you, your shoes were not worn out, your feet were not painfully hardened, these entire forty years!

You know in your heart, that as if any man should chastise his son, so the lord of the gods will chastise you. You will keep the commands of the lord of the gods, to follow his ways, and to fear him. For the lord of the gods will bring you into a good and extensive land, where there are torrents of waters, and fountains issuing of deep places through the plains and the mountains. A land of wheat and barley, in which are vines, figs, pomegranates. A land of olive oil and honey. A land on which you will not eat your bread with poverty, and you will not want anything. A land whose stones are iron, and out of its mountains you will dig brass. You will eat and be filled and will bless the lord of the gods on the good land, which he has given you. Pay attention to yourself that you don't forget the lord of the gods, and don't keep his commands, and his judgments, and ordinances, which I command you this day, in case when you have eaten and are full, and have built good houses, and lived in them, and your oxen and your sheep are multiplied to you, and your silver and your gold are multiplied to you, and all your possessions are multiplied to you, you should be exalted in heart, and forget the lord of the gods, who brought you out of the land of Egypt, out of the house of slavery, who brought you through that great and terrible wilderness, where is the biting serpent, and scorpion, and drought, where there was no water, who brought you a fountain of water out of the flinty rock, who fed you with manna in the wilderness, which you did not know, and your fathers did not know, that he might punish you, and thoroughly test you, and you'll do good in your latter days.

In case you should say in your heart, "My strength and the power of my hand have worked for me this great wealth." But you will remember the lord of the gods, that he gives you the strength to get wealth, so that he may establish his covenant, which the Lord swore to your fathers, and on this day. It will come to pass if you do at all forget the lord of the gods, and should go after other gods, and serve them, and worship them, I call the sky and earth to witness against you this day, that you will certainly perish. As also the other nations which the lord of the gods destroys in front of you, so will you perish, because you did not listen to the voice of the lord of the gods.

# CHAPTER 9

Listen Israel! You go this day across the Jordan to inherit nations greater and stronger than yourselves, cities great and walled up to the sky. A great people and many and tall, the sons of Anakites, whom you know. Regarding whom you have heard it said, "Who can stand before the children of Anakites?"

"You will know today, that Lord the god will go before you. He is a consuming fire, and he will destroy them, and he will turn them back before you and will destroy them quickly, as the Lord said to you, 'Don't say in your heart, when Lord the god has destroyed these nations in front of you, "Because of my righteousness, the Lord brought me in to inherit this good land." It is not for your righteousness, or the holiness of your heart, that you go in to inherit their land, but because of the wickedness of these nations that the Lord will destroy them from before you, so he that he may establish the covenant, which the Lord swore to our fathers, to Abraham, Isaac, and Jacob. You will know today, that it is not for your righteousness that Lord the god gives you this good land to inherit, for you are a stubborn people.'"

"Don't forget how much you provoked the lord of the gods in the wilderness, from the day that you came out of Egypt, even until you came into this place, you continued to be disobedient toward the Lord. Also in Horeb you provoked the Lord, and the Lord was angry enough with you to destroy

# CHAPTER 9

you. When I went up into the mountain to receive the tablets of stone, the tablets of the covenant, which the Lord made with you, and I was in the mountain forty days and forty nights, I ate no bread and drank no water. The Lord gave me the two tablets of stone written with the finger of God, and on them, there had been written all the words which the Lord spoke to you in the mountain on the day of the assembly. It happened after forty days and forty nights, the Lord gave me the two tablets of stone, the tablets of the covenant. The Lord said to me, "'Rise, go down quickly from here. Your people, whom you brought out of the land of Egypt, have transgressed. They have quickly abandoned the way which I commanded them, and have made themselves a molten image.'"

The Lord said to me, "I have said to you before, 'I have seen this people, and, look, it is a stubborn people. Now allow me to completely destroy them, and I will blot out their name from under the sky, and will make of you a nation great and strong, and more numerous than this.'"

"I turned and went down from the mountain, and the mountain burned with fire to the sky, and the two tablets of the testimonies were in my two hands. When I saw that you had sinned against the lord of the gods, and had made for yourselves a molten image, and had gone astray from the way, which the Lord commanded you to do, I took hold of the two tablets, and threw them out of my two hands, and broke them before you. I made my petition before the Lord as also in the first forty days and forty nights. I ate no bread and drank no water, on account of all your sins which you sinned in doing evil before the lord of the gods to provoke him. I was greatly terrified because of the rage and anger because the Lord was provoked with you completely to the point of destroying you, yet the Lord listened to me at this time also. He was angry enough with Aaron to destroy him completely, and I prayed for Aaron also at that time. Your sin which you had made, the calf, I took, and burnt it with fire, and pounded it and ground it down until it became fine, and it became like dust, and I threw the dust into the brook that descended from the mountain."

Also at Burning, and at Temptation, and at the Graves of Desire, you provoked the Lord. When the Lord sent you out from Kadesh Barnea, saying, "Go up and inherit the land which I give to you," then you disobeyed the word of the lord of the gods, and did not believe him, and did not listen to his voice. You were disobedient towards the Lord from the day in which he became known to you.

I prayed before the Lord forty days and forty nights, the number that I prayed before, for the Lord said that he would completely destroy you. I prayed to god, and said, "Lord Ba'al, King of gods,[1] don't destroy your people and your inheritance, who you did redeem, who you brought out of the land of Egypt with your great power, and with your strong hand, and with your high arm. Remember Abraham, Isaac, and Jacob your servants, to whom you swore by yourself. Look not at the hardness of heart of these people, and their impieties, and their sins. In case the inhabitants of the land

# CHAPTER 9

from where you brought us out say, 'Because the Lord could not bring them into the land of which he told them, and because he hated them, has he brought them out to slay them in the wilderness.' These are your people and your portion, who you brought out of the land of Egypt with your great strength, and with your mighty hand, and with your high arm."

## CHAPTER 9 NOTES

**1** Codex Vaticanus: KE basileu tōn ṯeōn ( K̄E͞BACIΛEYTⲰNⲐEⲰN). Translation: Lord king of the gods

• Codex Alexandrinus: kurie kurie basileu tōn ṯeōn (KYPIE KYPIE BACIΛEYTⲰNⲐEⲰN). Translation: lord lord king of the gods

• Septuagint manuscript 799: Kurie kurie basileus tōn etnōn (Kυβιϭ ⲗυβιϭ υⲗⲟⲧⲗⲟⲩⲥ τῶͻ ϭθνⲟⲟⲩ). Translation: Lord lord king of the nations

• Septuagint manuscript 707: Kurie kurie basileus tōn aiōnōn (Kυβιϭ ⲗυβιϭ υⲗⲟⲧⲗⲟⲩⲥ τῶͻ α/ⲟⲟͻⲟⲟⲩ). Translation: Lord lord king of the ages (or centuries)

• Leningrad Codex: 'ădōnāy Yəhwih (אֲדֹנָי יְהוִה). Translation: my Lord Yehwih

• Peshitta: mryå ålhå ll (ܠܠ ܐܠܗܐ ܡܪܝܐ). Translation: lord god of night (or Lil)

• Targum Onkelos: Yəyā 'ĕlāhîm (יְיָ אֱלָהִים). Translation: Yahweh gods

• Targum Pseudo-Jonathan: Yəyā 'ĕlāhākôn (יְיָ אֱלָהְכוֹן). Translation: Yahweh your gods

# CHAPTER 9

• Sahidic manuscript 17: pjoeis pjoeis prro nnnoute (ⲡⲭⲟⲉⲓⲥ ⲡⲭⲟⲉⲓⲥ ⲡⲣⲣⲟ ⲛⲛⲛⲟⲩⲧⲉ). Translation: the master (or mistress) the master (or mistress) the Ra (or sun) of the god (or divinity)

• Sahidic manuscript 2006: pjoeis pjoeis prro pnoute (ⲡⲭⲟⲉⲓⲥ ⲡⲭⲟⲉⲓⲥ ⲡⲣⲣⲟ ⲡⲛⲟⲩⲧⲉ). Translation: the master (or mistress) the master (or mistress) the Ra (or sun) of god (or divinity)

This verse has not survived among the Dead Sea Scrolls. The differences between these two verses show a clear difference between the Aramaic text the Greeks translated circa 250 BCE, and the Hebrew text the Masoretes began copying them in the 4th century CE. The removal of references to other gods is consistent with the Hasmonean redaction.

The term 'King of the Gods' is clearly polytheistic, which points to this section of *Deuteronomy* being older than *Leviticus*, which was essentially monotheistic. In the Canaanite religion, which El was central to, Ba'al Hadad became the King of the Gods after El left the world, and this verse seems to be about him. Lord Lord (Κυριε Κυριε) appears to be a Greek translation of ådn bôlå (אלעב ןדא) meaning Lord Ba'al. The term King of the Gods would have been mlkå hålhyn (ןיהלא אכלמ) in Aramaic, meaning the line would have read ådn bôlå mlkå hålhyn, which would be translated as Lord Ba'al King of the Elohim in Hebrew, which would have certainly been removed by a Hasmonean redactor.

The general implication of this line is that Lord Ba'al was the Lord speaking to Moses according to the author, and that he was also called the King of the Gods, which would indicate the author was familiar with the Ba'al Cycle, and he expected his readers to also be familiar with it. Both the prophets Hosea and Zephaniah denounced the Israelite worship of Ba'al, along with other gods. Hosea lived in Samaria before it was conquered by the Assyrians, while Zephaniah

# CHAPTER 9

lived in Judah during the time of Josiah, shortly before Egypt conquered Judah.

The Samaritan prophet Ezekiel, who lived before King Josiah's reforms, prophesied on behalf of Lord Ba'al (Κυριε Κυριε), whom he identified as coming from Zephon, where Ba'al Hadad's temple was built in the Ugaritic Texts, and denounced the worship of the gods of the Temple of Jerusalem, suggesting that worship of Lord Ba'al was widespread at the time. The inclusion of the term 'King of the gods' suggests that Lord Ba'al was also the god the Ammonites called Milkam (𐤌𐤋𐤊𐤌), which the author of *4ᵗʰ Kingdoms* (Masoretic *Kings*) called "King" (מלך), transliterated as Molok̆ (Μολοχ) in the Septuagint, and accented as Mōlek (מֹלֶךְ) by the Masoretes, whom the Judahites were recorded as sacrificing their firstborn to before King Josiah's reforms. This supports the origin of *Deuteronomy* in the Kingdom of Samaria before it was conquered by the Assyrians, and the book's usage in Judah before the reforms.

Ba'al Hammon continued to be worshiped as the king of the gods in Carthage and Iberia until the Romans conquered the Carthaginians. His name was derived from the Egyptian god Amen, suggesting a later interpretation of the Ba'al in *Deuteronomy*. Like Moses' god, Ba'al Hammon required the sacrifice of the firstborn, of both humans and animals, although according to Roman records the rich could substitute slaves. Unlike Moses' laws, where the firstborn was cut up and sacrificed on an altar at a bamah, the Carthaginians cooked Ba'al Hammon's victims alive in a bronze cauldron. This is likely the origin of Josiah's ban on the sacrifices to Molek, which are also described as being burned in fire.

# CHAPTER 10

At that time the Lord said to me, "Cut for yourself two stone tablets like the first, and come up to me in the mountain, and make for yourself a wooden box.[1] You will write on the tablets the words which were on the first tablets which you broke, and you will put them into the box."

So I made a box of boards of incorruptible wood, and I cut tablets of stone like the first, and I went up to the mountain, and the two tablets were in my hand. He wrote on the tablets like the first, writing the ten commandments, which the Lord spoke to you in the mountain out of the middle of the fire, and the Lord gave them to me. I turned and came down from the mountain, and I put the tablets into the box which I had made, and they were there, as the Lord commanded me.

The children of Israel departed from Beeroth of the sons of Jaakan to Mosera, where Aaron died, and there he was buried, and Eleazar his son became priest in his place. They departed there to Gudgodah and traveled from Gudgodah to Jotbath, a land in which are torrents of water. At that time the Lord separated the tribe of Levi, to carry the box of the covenant of the Lord, and to stand near before the Lord and minister and bless in his name until this day. Therefore the Levites have no part of the inheritance among their brothers. The Lord himself is their inheritance, as he said to them. I stood on the mount forty days and forty nights, and the Lord heard me at that time also, and the Lord would not destroy you.

The Lord said to me, "Go, set out before these people, and let them go in and inherit the land, which I swore to their fathers to give to them."

Now, Israel, what does the lord of the gods require of you, except to fear the lord of the gods, and to follow all his ways, and to love him, and to serve the lord of the gods with all your heart, and with all your mind, to keep the commandments of the lord of the gods, and his ordinances, all that I order you today, that it may go well with you? See your lord, the god Shamayim. The skies of Shamayim and the earth, and everything on it are his.[2] Only the Lord chose your fathers to love them, and he chose their descendants after them, including you, above all nations, like today. Therefore you will circumcise the hardness of your heart, and you will not harden your neck.

The lord of the gods is God of gods, and the Lord of lords, the great, and strong, and terrible God, who does not wonder at persons, nor will he by any means accept a bribe. Executing judgment for the stranger and orphan and widow, and he loves the stranger and gives him food and clothing. You will love the stranger, for you were strangers in the land of Egypt. You will fear the lord of the gods, and serve him, and will cleave to him, and will swear by his name. He is your pride, and he is your god, who has worked among you these great and glorious things, which your eyes have seen. With seventy minds your fathers went down into Egypt, but the

# CHAPTER 10

lord of the gods has made you as the stars of the sky in multitude.

## CHAPTER 10 NOTES

**1** Codex Vaticanus: kibōton (ⲕⲓⲃⲱⲧⲟⲛ). Translation: box

• Leningrad Codex: 'ărôn (אָרֹן). Translation: cupboard (or closet, cabinet)

• Shapira scrolls: årn (𐤀𐤓𐤍). Translation: box

• Peshitta: qbwrtå (ܩܒܘܪܬܐ). Translation: coffin (or urn, sarcophagus)

• Targum Onkelos: 'ărônā' (אֲרוֹנָא). Translation: cupboard (or closet, cabinet)

• Targum Pseudo-Jonathan: 'ărônā' (אֲרוֹנָא). Translation: cupboard (or closet, cabinet)

• Sahidic manuscript 17: kibōtos (ⲕⲓⲃⲱⲧⲟⲥ). Translation: box

**2** Codex Vaticanus: idou $\overline{KS}$ o $\overline{TS}$ sou o $\overline{OUNOS}$ kai o $\overline{OUNOS}$ tou $\overline{OUNOU}$, ē gē kai panta, osa estin en autē (ⲓⲇⲟⲩⲕⲥⲟⲑⲉⲥⲥⲟⲩⲟⲟⲩⲛⲟⲥ ⲕⲁⲓⲟⲟⲩⲛⲟⲥⲧⲟⲩⲟⲩⲛⲟⲩ ⲏⲅⲏⲕⲁⲓ ⲡⲁⲛⲧⲁ ⲟⲥⲁ ⲉⲥⲧⲓⲛ ⲉⲛ ⲁⲩⲧⲏ). Translation: "See Lord the god of your vaulted-sky (or Uranus), and the vaulted-sky (or Uranus) of the vaulted-sky (or Uranus), the earth (or Ge) and everything there are his."

• Septuagint manuscript 767: idou kuriou tou ṯeou sou ouranos kai uranos tou ouranou, ē gē kai panta, osa estin en autē (ⲓⲇⲟⲩ ⲕⲩⲣⲓⲟⲩ ⲧⲟ ⲑⲑⲟⲩ ⲥⲟⲩ ⲟⲩⲣⲁⲛⲟⲥ ⲕⲁⲓ ⲩⲣⲁⲛⲟⲥ ⲧⲟ ⲟⲩⲣⲁⲛⲟⲩ, ⲏ ⲅⲏ ⲕⲁⲓ ⲡⲁⲛⲧⲁ, ⲟⲥⲁ ⲉⲥⲧⲓⲛ ⲉⲛ ⲁⲩⲧⲏ). Translation: "See Lord the god of you, and Uranus of the skies of Uranus, the earth and everything there are his."

# CHAPTER 10

- Septuagint manuscript 318: idou kuriou tou ṯeou sou ouranos tou ouranou, ē gē kai panta, osa estin en autē (ⲓⲇⲟⲩ ⲕⲩⲣⲓⲟⲩ ⲧⲱ θ丂ⲟⲩ ⲥⲟⲩ ⲟⲩⲣ⳽ⲛⲟⲥ ⲧⲱ ⲟⲩⲣ⳽ⲛⲟⲩ, ⳽ ⲅⳑ �034⳽ⲓ πⲇ�726⳽, ⲟⳝ⳽ 丂ⳡⲓⲛ ⳽ⲛ ⲇⲩⲧⳑ). Translation: "See Lord thegod of you, skies of sky, the earth and everything there are his."

- Septuagint manuscript 83: idou kuriou tou ṯeou sou kai ta dikaeōmata autou osa egō entellomai soi sēmeron o ouranos kai o ouranos tou ouranou, ē gē kai panta, osa estin en autē (ⲓⲇⲟⲩ ⲕⲩⲣⲓⲟⲩ ⲧⲱ θ丂ⲟⲩ ⲥⲟⲩ ⳽ⳁ ⲧⳛ 丂ⲓⲗⳁⲟⲟⲩⳑ⳽ⲧⳛ ⳽ⲩⲧ⳽ ⲟ⳽⳽ 丂ⲅ⳽⳽ ⳽ⲧⲗ丂ⳛⳑⳁ 丂θ 丂ⳑⲩⲣ⳽ ⲟ ⲟⲩⲣ⳽ⲛⲟⲥ ⳽ⳁ ⲟ ⲟⲩⲣ⳽ⲛⲟⲥ ⲧⲱ ⲟⲩⲣ⳽ⲛⲟⲩ, ⳽ ⲅⳑ ⳽⳽ πⲇ�30⳽, ⳽ ⲅⳑ 丂ⳡⲓⲛ ⳽ⲛ ⲇⲩⲧⳑ). Translation: "See Lord thegod of you, and the authority of his as far as I declare to you today, the skies and the skies of the sky, the earth and everything there are his."

- Dead Sea Scroll 4QDeut[l]: the verse is damaged, however -hârṣ wkl âš- (-אש כול והארץ-) survives. Translation: "-land and everything-"

- Leningrad Codex: hēn laYhwâ 'ĕlōhêkā haššāmayim ûšəmê haššāmāyim hā'āreṣ wəkol-'ăšer-bāh. (הֵן לַיהֹוָה אֱלֹהֶיךָ הַשָּׁמַיִם וּשְׁמֵי הַשָּׁמָיִם הָאָרֶץ וְכׇל־אֲשֶׁר־בָּהּ). Translation: "see the Yahweh your god Shamayim and the sky of Shamayim the earth and everything in her."

- Peshitta: dmryâ ânwn âlhk šmyâ wšmy šmyâ wârôâ wkl dâyt bh (ⲇⲙⲣⲓ⳽ ⲁⲛⲱⲛ ⲁⲗⲏⲕ ⲥⲙⲓ⳽ ⲱⲥⲙⲓ ⲥⲙⲓ⳽ ⲱⲁⲣⲟⲁ ⲱⲕⲗ ⲇⲁⲩⲧ ⲃⲏ). Translation: master of ours, our god Shamyya (or sky) and name Shamyya (or sky) and land and everything that exists in it

- Targum Onkelos: hā' daYyā 'ĕlāhāk šəmayyā' ûšəmê šəmayyā' 'ar'ā' wəkol dî bah (הָא דַּייָ אֱלָהָךְ שְׁמַיָּא וּשְׁמֵי שְׁמַיָּא אַרְעָא וְכָל דִּי בַהּ). Translation: see the Yahweh, your god sky (or Shemayyah), land, and everything in it

- Targum Pseudo-Jonathan: hā' daYyā 'ĕlāhākôn šəmaya' ûšəmê šəmaya' wəkittê mal'ākaya' dibhôn limšamšĭn qŏdāmôy 'ar'ā' wəkol

הָא דְיָי אֱלָהְכוֹן שְׁמַיָּא וּשְׁמֵי שְׁמַיָּא וְכִתֵּי מַלְאָכַיָּא דְּבְהוֹן לִמְשַׁמְשִׁין bāh də'ît
(קֳדָמוֹי אַרְעָא וְכָל דְּאִית בָּהּ). Translation: Translation: see the Yahweh,
your godssky (or Shemayyah) and the name Shemeyyah (or sky),
land, and chicken-messenger (possibly the peacock-angel), their
bear, the servants of ancient land and everything in it

• Sahidic manuscript 17: eis tpe tapjoeis peknoute te auō tpe ntpe
auō pkah mn nka nim etšoop nhētou (ⲉⲓⲥ ⲧⲡⲉ ⲧⲁⲡϫⲟⲉⲓⲥ
ⲡⲉⲕⲛⲟⲩⲧⲉ ⲧⲉ ⲁⲩⲱ ⲧⲡⲉ ⲛⲧⲡⲉ ⲁⲩⲱ ⲡⲕⲁϩ ⲙⲛ ⲛⲕⲁ ⲛⲓⲙ
ⲉⲧϣⲟⲟⲡ ⲛϩⲏⲧⲟⲩ). Translation: See above the horn of the master (or
mistress) of the god (of divine) of you and the sky of the sky and
the land and everything existing in them.

• Sahidic manuscript 2048: eis tpe tapjoeis peknoute te auō tpe mn
ntpe auō pkah mn nka nim etšoop nhētou (ⲉⲓⲥ ⲧⲡⲉ ⲧⲁⲡϫⲟⲉⲓⲥ
ⲡⲉⲕⲛⲟⲩⲧⲉ ⲧⲉ ⲁⲩⲱ ⲧⲡⲉ ⲙⲛ ⲛⲧⲡⲉ ⲁⲩⲱ ⲡⲕⲁϩ ⲙⲛ ⲛⲕⲁ ⲛⲓⲙ
ⲉⲧϣⲟⲟⲡ ⲛϩⲏⲧⲟⲩ). Translation: See above the horn of the master (or
mistress) of the god (of divine) of you and in the sky of the sky and
the land and everything existing in them.

The difference between the Septuagint's version and the
Masoretic version of this verse is significant, and the Septuagint's
reading is generally used by translators of the Masoretic Text. The
Greek translation is consistent with the Greek concept of the sky
circa 250 BCE, wherein there was a sky under the vaulted dome
covering the earth, above which lived the gods. This structure is
similar to the Second Temple Era description of the vaulted sky
found in the Books of Enoch, except there were seven skies in the
Jewish version, one above the other. This seven-skied world was
drawn from the concept of the celestial spheres, in which each
visible planet moved in its own spherical sky.

As there is no evidence of the Israelites ever believing in a single
vaulted sky, the Septuagint's version is likely a Greek
reinterpretation that assumed the word wšmy (וּשְׁמִי) was a

transcription error. If the Masoretic version is similar to what the Greeks translated, it appears to be a partial redaction of a version of *Deuteronomy* in which Shamayim was the Lord. This would point clearly to *Deuteronomy's* composition in Samaria under Assyrian rule, as the Canaanite god Shamayim was regarded as the local variant of Asshur, the national god of Assyria, who by that time was known as to Ansar (⊶⊦⊲), the "Whole Sky." It cannot be determined from this fragment in the Masoretic Text if the original author was a Shamayim worshiper, or if an older text had Shamayim's name inserted, however, the worship of Shamayim was widespread in Samaria and Judah in the 8$^{th}$ and 7$^{th}$ centuries BCE, as reported by Hosea, Zephaniah, and Jonah. King Josiah ultimately banned the worship of Shamayim in Judah circa 625 BCE.

# CHAPTER 11

You will love the lord of the gods and will follow his appointments, and his ordinances, and his commandments, and his judgments, always. You will know today, for I speak not to your children, who don't know and have not seen the discipline of the lord of the gods, and his wonderful works, and his strong hand, and his high arm, and his miracles, and his wonders, which he worked in Egypt against Pharaoh king of Egypt, and all his land, and what he did to the army of the Egyptians, and their chariots, and their cavalry, and their infantry. How he made the water of the Papyrus Sea to overwhelm the face of them as they pursued after you, and the Lord destroyed them until today. All the things which he did to you in the wilderness until you came into this place, and all the things that he did to Dathan and Abiram the sons of Eliab the son of Reuben, whom the earth opening her mouth swallowed up, and their houses, and their tents, and all their substance that was with them among all Israel. For your eyes have seen all the mighty works of the Lord, which he worked among you today.

You will keep all his commandments, all I command you today, that you may live, and be multiplied, and that you may go in and inherit the land, into which you go across the Jordan to inherit, so you may live long on the land, which the Lord swore to your fathers to give to them, and to their seed after them, a land flowing with milk and honey.

# CHAPTER 11

The land into which you go to inherit is not like the land of Egypt, where you came out of, where they sow the seed, and water it with their feet, as a garden of plants. The land into which you go to inherit is a land of mountains and plains, it will drink the rainwater from the sky. A land which the the lord of the gods surveys continually, the eyes of the lord of the gods are on it from the beginning of the year to the end of the year. Now if you will indeed listen to all the commands which I order you today, to love the lord of the gods, and to serve him with all your heart, and with all your mind, then he will give to your land the early and late rain in its season, and you will bring in your grain, and your wine, and your oil. He will give food in your fields to your livestock, and when you have eaten and are full, pay attention to yourself that your heart does not be puffed up, and you transgress, and serve other gods, and worship them. The Lord will be angry with you, and hold back the sky, and there will not be rain, and the earth will not yield its fruit. You will perish quickly from off the good land, which the Lord has given you.

You will keep these words in your heart and your mind, and you will bind them as a sign on your hand, and it will be fixed before your eyes. You will teach them to your children, to speak about them when you sit in the house, and when you walk, and when you sleep, and when you rise. You will write them on the lintels of your houses, and your gates, that your days may be long, and the days of your children, in the land which the Lord swore to your fathers to give to them, as the days of the sky on the earth. It will come to pass, that if you will indeed listen to all these commands, which I order you to observe today, to love our lord of the gods, and to follow all his ways, and to cling close to him, then the Lord will throw out all these nations before you, and you will inherit great nations, stronger than yourselves. Every place on which the sole of your foot will tread will be yours, from the wilderness and Anti-lebanon, and the great river, the river Euphrates, even as far as the west sea will be your frontiers. No one will stand before you, and the lord of the gods will put the fear of you and the dread of you on the face of all the land, in which you will tread, as he told you.

See, I set before you today the blessing and the curse, the blessing, if you listen to the commands of the lord of the gods, all that I command you today, and the curse if you do not listen to the commands of our lord of the gods, all I command you today, and you wander from the way which I have commanded you, having gone to serve other gods, which you don't know. It will come to pass when the lord of the gods has brought you into the land into which you go over to inherit it, then you will put a blessing on Mount Gerizim, and a curse on Mount Ebal. See! Are not these beyond the Jordan, to the west in the land of Canaan, which lies near the circle[1] by the high oak? For you are passing over the Jordan, to go in and inherit the land, which our lord of the gods gives you to inherit always, and you will live in it. You will pay attention to do all his ordinances, and these judgments, as many as I set before you today.

# CHAPTER 11

## CHAPTER 11 NOTES

**1** Codex Vaticanus: Golgol (ܪܘܠܪܘܠ)

- Codex Colberto-Sarravianus: Golgōn (ܪܘܠܪܘܢ)
- Codex Ambrosiano A 147: Golgod (ܪܘܠܪܘܕ)
- Codex Venetus: Godgod (ܪܘܕܪܘܕ)
- Septuagint manuscript 407: Golgōd (Γολγωδ)
- Septuagint manuscript 82: Golgō (Γολγω)
- Septuagint manuscript 630: Golgon (Γολγⲱ)
- Septuagint manuscript 58: Galgal (Γαλγαλ)
- Septuagint manuscript 321: Goggol (Γογγολ)
- Septuagint manuscript 75: Golgol (Γολγολ)
- Dead Sea Scroll 1QDeutᵃ: glgl (𐤂𐤋𐤂𐤋). Translation: circle
- Leningrad Codex: gilgāl (גִּלְגָּל). Translation: circle
- Shapira scrolls: glgl (𐤂𐤋𐤂𐤋). Translation: circle
- Peshitta: Glôlå (ܓܠܘܠܐ)
- Targum Onkelos: Gilgǝlā' (גִּלְגְּלָא)
- Targum Pseudo-Jonathan: Gūlgǝlā' (גּוּלְגְּלָא)
- Sahidic manuscript 17: Golgol ( Ⲅⲟⲗⲅⲟⲗ)

This was generally assumed to be a reference to a town in previous centuries, however, archaeologists have discovered several ceremonial stone circles in Canaan that were used between 1200 and 1000 BCE for gatherings that are assumed to be religious in nature. As these stone circles are found down in the valleys, unlike the bamah altars at the tops of hills where the Canaanites worshiped, and "circles" (נלגל) are mentioned throughout the old Hebrew texts, it is assumed they are early Israelite religious centers from before the First Temple was built.

# CHAPTER 12

These are the ordinances and the judgments, which you will observe and do in the land, which the lord of the gods of your fathers gives you for an inheritance, all the days which you live on the land. You will completely destroy all the places in which they served their gods in the land you inherit, on the high mountains and the hills, and under the thick tree. You will destroy their altars, and break to pieces their pillars, and you will cut down their groves, and you will burn with fire the carved images of their gods, and you will abolish their name out of that place. You will not do so to the lord of the gods, but in the place which the lord of the gods will choose, in one of your cities to name his name there, and to be called on, you will even seek him out and go there.

You will take there your whole burnt offerings, and your sacrifices, and your first fruits, and your vows, and your freewill offerings, and your offerings of thanksgiving, the firstborn of your herds, and your flocks. You will eat there before the lord of the gods, and you will rejoice in all the things on which you will lay your hand, you and your houses, as the lord of the gods has blessed you. You will not do altogether as we do here today, every man doing what is pleasing in his own sight. Until now you have not arrived at your rest and the inheritance, which our lord of the gods gives you. You will go over the Jordan and will live in the land, which our lord of the gods takes as an inheritance for you.

He will give you rest from all your enemies, and you will live safely. There will be a place which the lord of the gods will choose for his name to be called there, there will you bring all things that I order you today, your whole burnt offerings, and your sacrifices, and your tithes, and the first fruits of your hands, and every choice gift of yours, whatever you will vow to the lord of the gods. You will rejoice before the lord of the gods, you and your sons, and your daughters, and your men-servants and your woman-slaves, and the Levite that is at your gates, because he has no portion or inheritance with you. Pay attention to yourself that you don't offer your whole burnt offerings in any place which you will see, except in the place which the lord of the gods will choose. In one of your tribes, there you will offer your whole burnt offerings, and there you will do all things whatever I order you today.

You will kill according to all your desire and will eat flesh according to the blessing of the lord of the gods, which he has given you in every city, the unclean that are with you, and the clean will eat it on equal terms, like the doe or the stag. Only, you will not eat the blood, you will pour it out on the ground like water. In your cities, you will not be able to eat the tithe of your grain, and your wine, and of your oil, the firstborn of your herd and of your flock, and all your vows as many as you have vowed, and your thanks-offerings, and the first fruits of your hands. Before the lord of the gods, you will eat it, in the place which the lord of the gods will choose for himself, you, and your son, and your daughter, your man-slave, and your woman-slave, and the stranger that is within your gates, and you will rejoice before the lord of the gods, on whatever you will lay your hand. Pay attention to yourself that you do not desert the Levites in all the time that you live on the earth.

If the lord of the gods expands your borders, as he said to you, and you will say, "I will eat flesh," if your mind should desire to eat flesh, you will eat all the flesh you desire in your mind. If the place that the lord of the gods will choose for himself where his name is called on, is far from you, then you will kill from your herd and of your flock which God has given you, even as I commanded you, and you will eat in your cities according to the desire of your mind. As the doe and the stag are eaten, so will you eat it, the unclean in you and the clean will eat it the same way. Pay diligent attention that you eat no blood, for blood is the life of it, and the life will not be eaten with the flesh. You will not eat it, you will pour it out on the ground like water. You will not eat it, that it may go well with you and with your sons after you if you will do that which is good and pleasing before the lord of the gods.

You will take your holy things, if you have any, and your vowed offerings, and come to the place which the lord of the gods will choose to have his name placed on it. You will sacrifice your whole burnt offerings, you will offer the flesh on the altar of the lord of the gods, but the blood of your sacrifices you will pour out at the foot of the altar of the lord of the gods, and the flesh you may eat. Beware and listen, and you will do all the commands which I order you, that it may go well with you and with your sons forever if you will do that which is pleasing and good before the lord of the gods. If the lord of the gods will completely destroy the nations from before you where you go to inherit their land, and you will inherit it and live in their land. Pay attention to yourself that you don't seek to follow them after they are destroyed before you, saying, "How do these nations worship their gods? I will do the same."

You will not do so to your god, for they have sacrificed among their gods, the abominations of the Lord which he hates, for they burn their sons and their daughters in the fire of their gods. Every word that I command you today, you will observe it: you will not add to it, nor take from it.

# CHAPTER 13

If there appears among you a prophet or one who dreams a dream, and he predicts a sign or a wonder, and the sign or the wonder happens as he told you, and he says, "Let's go and serve other gods," who you don't know. You will not listen to the words of that prophet, or the dreamer of that dream, because the lord of the gods tests you, to know whether you love your god with all your heart and with all your mind. You will obey the lord of the gods, and fear him, and you will hear his voice, and attach yourselves to him. That prophet or that dreamer of a dream will die, for he has spoken to make you error from the lord of the gods who brought you out of the land of Egypt, who redeemed you from slavery, to draw you away from the way that the lord of the gods commanded you to walk. You will abolish the evil from among you.

If your brother by your father or mother, or your son, or daughter, or your wife in your heart, or friend who is equal to your own mind, says to you secretly, "Let us go and serve other gods," which neither you nor your fathers have known, from the gods of the nations that are around you, whether they are from near you or at a distance from you, from one end of the earth to the other, you will not agree with him, neither will you listen to him. Your eye will not spare him, and you will feel no regret for him, nor will you at all protect him. You will certainly report concerning him, and your hands will be on him among the first to slay him, and the hands of all the people will follow. They will stone him with stones, and he will die, because he wanted to draw you away from the lord of the gods who brought you out of the land of Egypt, out of the house of slavery.

All Israel will hear, and fear, and will not again do this evil thing among you. If in one of your cities which the lord of the gods gives you to live in, you hear men saying, "Evil men have gone out from you, and have caused all the inhabitants of their land to fall away, saying, 'Let us go and worship other gods,' whom you did not know, then you will inquire and ask, and search diligently, and look, if it is clearly true, and this abomination has taken place among you, you will completely destroy all the residents in that land with the edge of the sword. You will solemnly curse it, and all things in it. All its spoils you will gather into its public roads, and you will burn the city with fire, and all its spoils publicly before the lord of the gods. It will remain uninhabited forever, and it will not be built again. There will be none of the cursed thing left in your hand that the Lord may turn from his fierce anger, and give you mercy and pity you, and multiply you, as he swore to your father, if you listen to the voice of the lord of the gods, to keep his commandments, all that I order you today, to do that which is good and pleasing before the lord of the gods.

# CHAPTER 14

You are the children of the lord of the gods. You will not shave any baldness between your eyes for the dead. For you are a holy people to the lord of the gods, and the lord of the gods has chosen you to be a unique people to himself of all the nations on the face of the earth. You will not eat any abominable thing. These are the beasts which you will eat: the calf from the corral, the lamb from the herd, the goat kid, the red deer, the gazelle, the antelope, the wild donkey,[1] and white-tail,[2] and oryx,[3] and giraffe.[4] Every animal that has split-hoofs, and makes claws of two divisions, and that chews the cud among beasts, these you will eat. These you will not eat from these that chew the cud, and of those that divide the hoofs, and make distinct claws: the camel, and the hare, and the rabbit, because they chew the cud, but do not have divided-hoofs, so these are unclean to you. As for the swine, because they have divided hoofs and makes claws of the hoof, yet he does not chew the cud, it is unclean for you. You will not eat their flesh, or touch their dead bodies.

These you may eat of all that are in the water. You may eat all that have fins and scales. All that do not have fins and scales you will not eat, as they are unclean for you. You may eat every clean bird. These of the birds you may not eat: the eagle, and the bearded vulture, and the sea-eagle, and the vulture, and the kite and these like them, and the sparrow, and the owl, and the seagull, and the heron, and the swan,

# Chapter 14

and the stork, and the cormorant, and the hawk, and similar to them, and the hoopoe, and the raven, and the pelican, and the heron and those like them, and the flamingo and the bat. All winged animals that creep are unclean to you, and you will not eat them. You may eat every clean bird. You will eat nothing that spontaneously dies; it will be given to the traveler in your cities and he will eat it, or you will sell it to a stranger because you are a holy people to the lord of the gods.

You will not boil a lamb in his mother's milk. You will tithe a tenth of all the produce of your seed, the fruit of your field year by year. You will eat it in the place which the lord of the gods will choose to have his name called there, you will bring the tithe of your grain and your wine, and your oil, the firstborn of your herd and your flock, that you may learn to fear the lord of the gods always. If the journey is too far for you, and you are not able to bring them, because the place is far from you which the lord of the gods will choose to have his name called there, because the lord of the gods will bless you, then you will sell them for silver, and you will take the silver in your hands, and you will go to the place which the lord of the gods will choose. You will give the silver for whatever your mind will desire, for oxen or sheep, or wine, or you will lay it out on strong drink, or on whatever your mind may desire, and you will eat there before the lord of the gods, and you will rejoice and your house, and the Levite that is in your cities, because he has no portion or inheritance with you. After three years you will bring out all the tithes of your fruits, in that year you will lay it up in your cities. The Levites will come because they have no part or lot with you, and the stranger, and the orphan, and the widow which is in your cities. They will eat and be filled, that the lord of the gods may bless you in all the works which you will do.

## CHAPTER 14 NOTES

**1** Codex Vaticanus: tragelafon (ⲧⲣⲁⲅⲉⲗⲁⲫⲟⲛ). Translation: goat-deer

- Leningrad Codex: 'aqqô (אַקֹּו).

- Peshitta: yŏlå (ܝܥܠܐ). Translation: ibex

- Targum Onkelos: ya'lā' (יַעְלָא). Translation: ibex

- Targum Pseudo-Jonathan: ya'älîn (יַעְלִין). Translation: ibexes

- Sahidic manuscript 17: tragelafos (ⲧⲣⲁⲅⲉⲗⲁⲫⲟⲥ). Translation: goat-deer

The Greek translation uses the name tragelaphus, which was a mythical animal in Greek writing that Aristotle used as an example a thing that was knowable even though it did not exist. The term used in the Leningrad Codex is not proper Hebrew, but is accepted as referring to a wild goat. The Masoretic term was likely a transliteration of the Akkadian cuneiform word akanu (𒀭𒈨𒌷), meaning wild donkey.

**2** Codex Vaticanus: pugargon (ⲡⲩⲅⲁⲣⲅⲟⲛ). Translation: white-tail

- Codex Alexandrinus: pudargon (ⲡⲩⲇⲁⲣⲅⲟⲛ)

- Septuagint manuscript 509: purargon (πυβαργῳ)

- Septuagint manuscript 407: pugagron (πυγαγβῳ)

- Septuagint manuscript 319: pugarron (πυββῳ)

- Septuagint manuscript 52: pugaron (πυγᵃ⳹⊕)
- Septuagint manuscript 458: purgargon (πυρᵃ⳹γ⊕)
- Septuagint manuscript 318: purtagon (πυρτᴧγ⊕)
- Septuagint manuscript 529: pugarton (πυᵃ⳹τ⊕)
- Septuagint manuscript 500: purgalon (πυρᵧᵃᷓₒₙ)
- Septuagint manuscript 527: pelargon (πℓᵧₐᵣγ⊕)
- Leningrad Codex: dîšōn (דִּישֹׁן)
- Peshitta: rymå (ܪܝܡܐ). Translation: buffalo (or unicorn, Asian rhinoceros)
- Targum Onkelos: rêmā' (רֵימָא). Translation: buffalo (or unicorn, Asian rhinoceros)
- Targum Pseudo-Jonathan: rîmənîn (רֵימְנִין). Translation: buffaloes (or unicorns, Asian rhinoceroses)
- Sahidic manuscript 17: pugargon (ⲡⲩⲅⲁⲣⲅⲟⲛ). Translation: white-tail

The Greek term is a generic reference to a white-tail deer, however, the Masoretic term is less clear, as is does not appear to be Hebrew, Aramaic, or Akkadian. The closest term in the region is ḥiṣān (حِصَان) the Hijazi Arabic term for horse. As the Masoretic term is unclear, the Greek term is translated.

**3** Codex Vaticanus: oruga (ⲟⲣⲩⲅⲁ). Translation: oryx

- Septuagint manuscript 54: ogrega (ογρόγα)
- Leningrad Codex: tə'ô (תְאוֹ). Translation: buffalo
- Peshitta: dyså (ܕܝܣܐ)
- Targum Onkelos: tôrəbālā' (תּוֹרְבָלָא). Translation: auroch (or Lebanese buffalo)

130

- Targum Pseudo-Jonathan: tôrê bar (תּוֹרֵי בַּר). Translation: bollocks of the forest (or open space)
- Sahidic manuscript 17: oruga (ⲟⲣⲩⲅⲁ). Translation: oryx
- Sahidic manuscript 2006: not mentioned in the verse

**4** Codex Vaticanus: kamēlopardalin (ⲕⲁⲙⲏⲗⲟⲡⲁⲣⲇⲁⲁⲓⲛ). Translation: camel-leopard (or giraffe)

- Septuagint manuscript 54: kalopardalēn (κα/ϐπαρδαλω)
- Septuagint manuscript 72: kamēlopardalon (καμλ/ϐπαρδα/ϐν)
- Septuagint manuscript 29: kamēlopar̠talin (καμλ/ϐπαρθαλιν)
- Septuagint manuscript 509: kamēlonpardalin (καμλ/ϐνπαρδαλιν)
- Leningrad Codex: zāmer (זָמֶר). Translation: sing
- Peshitta: årnå (ܐܪܢܐ). Translation: mountain goat
- Targum Onkelos: dîṣā' (דִּיצָא)
- Targum Pseudo-Jonathan: dîsîn (דִּיצִין)
- Sahidic manuscript 17: kamēlopardalis (ⲕⲁⲙⲏⲗⲟⲡⲁⲣⲇⲁⲁⲗⲓⲥ). Translation: camel-leopard (or giraffe)

The Masoretic term zmr is generally accepted as being the same word as zmr (𐎏𐎎𐎗) in the Ugaritic, however, it is not clear which animal the word referred to. It is generally assumed to be some kind of antelope. As the Masoretic term is unclear, the Greek term is translated.

# CHAPTER 15

Every seven years you will have a general release. This is the ordinance of the release: you will remit every private debt which your neighbor owes you, and you will not ask payment of it from your brother, as it has been called a release by the lord of the gods. From a stranger, you will still ask whatever he has of yours, but for your brother, you will remit his debt to you. Doing this will ensure there will not be a poor person among you, for the lord of the gods will certainly bless you in the land which the lord of the gods gives you by inheritance, that you should inherit it.

If you will listen to the voice of the lord of the gods, to keep and do all these commandments, all I order you this day, (for the lord of the gods has blessed you in the way in which he spoke to you,) then you will lend to many nations, but you will not borrow, and you will rule over many nations, but they will not rule over you. If there is among you a poor man from your brothers in one of your cities in the land which the lord of the gods gives you, you will not harden your heart, nor will you close your hand from your brother who is in need. You will certainly open your hands to him and will lend to him as much as he wants according to his need. Pay attention to yourself, that there is not a secret thought in your heart thinking, "The seventh year, the year of release, draws near," and your eye will be evil to your brother that is in need, and you will not give to him, and he will cry against you to the Lord, and there will be a great sin in you. You will certainly give to him, and you will lend him as much as he wants, according to his need. You will not grudge in your heart as you give to him, because on this account the lord of the gods will bless you in all your works, and in all things on which you will lay your hand. The poor will never cease from your land, therefore I order you this, "You will certainly open your hands to your poor brother, and to he, that is distressed on your land. If your brother or sister, a Habiru or a female Habiru[1] is sold to you, they will serve you six years, and in the seventh year you will send him out free from you. When you send him out free from you, you will not send him out empty-handed. You will give him provision for the journey from your flock, grain, and wine. As the lord of the gods has blessed you, so you will give him. You will remember that you were a servant in the land of Egypt, and the lord of the gods redeemed you from there, therefore I order you to do this thing. If he should say to you, "I will not leave you," because he continues to love you and your house, as he is happy with you, then you will take a spike and pierce his ear through at the door, and he will be your servant forever. You will do the same with your woman-slave. It will not seem difficult for you when they are sent out free from you, because your servant has served you six years according to the annual hire of an employee, so the lord of the gods will bless you in all things whatever you may do.

Every firstborn that will be born among your cows and your sheep, you will sanctify the males to the lord of the gods, you will not work with your firstborn calf, and you will not shear the firstborn of your sheep. You will eat it before the Lord year after year in the place which the lord of the gods will choose, you and your house. If there is in it an imperfection, if it is lame or blind, an evil imperfection, you will not sacrifice it to the lord of the gods. You will eat it in your cities, the unclean in you and the clean will eat it as equals, like the doe or the stag. Only you will not eat the blood, you will pour it out on the earth like water.

## CHAPTER 15 NOTES

**1** Codex Vaticanus: Ebraeos cae Ēebraea (ЄΒΡΑΙΟΣ ΚΑΙ ΗЄΒΡΑΙΑ). Translation: Hebrew and the Hebrewess

• Codex Colberto-Sarravianus: Ebraeos ē Ēbraea (ЄΒΡΑΙΟΣ Η ΗΒΡΑΙΑ). Translation: Hebrew or Hebrewess

• Codex Venetus: Ebraios ē Ebraea (ЄΒΡΑΙΟΣ Η ЄΒΡΑΙΑ). Translation: Hebrew or Hebrewess

• Septuagint manuscript 76: Ebraios ē Ēebaia (Ευβαιος η Ηϭυαια). Translation: Ebraeos or the Hebrewess

• Septuagint manuscript 376: Ebeos ē Ēebraia (Ευϭος η Ηϭυβαια). Translation: Ebeos or the Hebrewess

• Septuagint manuscript 616: Ebaios ē Ēebraia (Ευαιος η Ηϭυβαια). Translation: Ebeos or the Hebrewess

• Leningrad Codex: hā'Ibrî 'ô hā'Ibriyyâ (הָעִבְרִי אוֹ הָעִבְרִיָּה). Translation: the Hebrew (or Eberite, crosser) or the Hebrewess (or Eberitess, female-crosser)

• Peshitta: Ôbryå åw Ôbrytå (ܥܒܪܝܐ ܐܘ ܥܒܪܝܬܐ). Translation: Hebrew or Hebrewess

- Targum Onkelos: bar Yiśrā'ēl 'ô bat Yiśrā'ēl (בַּר יִשְׂרָאֵל אוֹ בַּת יִשְׂרָאֵל). Translation: sons of Israel or daughters of Israel

- Targum Pseudo-Jonathan: bar Yiśrā'ēl 'ô bat Yiśrā'ēl (בַּר יִשְׂרָאֵל אוֹ בַת יִשְׂרָאֵל). Translation: sons of Israel or daughters of Israel

- Sahidic manuscript 17: nHebraios ē tHebraia (ⲛ2ⲉⲃⲣⲁⲓⲟⲥ ⲏ ⲧ2ⲉⲃⲣⲁⲓⲁ). Translation: Hebrews and Hebrewesses

The Eberites were the descendants of the patriarch Eber, an ancestor of Abraham who lived in Ur, in southern Iraq, according to Genesis. Many Semitic nations were believed to have been his descendants, including the Arameans, suggesting that this section of text was added during the early Iron Age, when Samaria ruled Aram. The term ôbr (עבר / עֲבַר) means 'to cross over' in both Hebrew and Aramaic, indicating that these Eberites were the people otherwise known to the Mesopotamians and Egyptians as Habiru. The earliest surviving mention of the Ḵabiru (𒄩𒁉𒊒), was from the time of King Rim-Sin I of Larsa between approximately 1822 and 1763 BCE, who reported they were an Aramean tribe living in southern Iraq.

Over the next 600 years, they were reported in hundreds of surviving documents ranging across the Middle East and Egypt, generally as marauders, although some were reported to be mercenaries, and those in Egypt were generally slaves. They disappeared around the end of the Bronze Age, shortly before the era of the Samaritan Empire that briefly controlled the Aramean cities of Damascus and Hama. As this reference is to the Habirus, that name is restored in this text. As there is no common feminine form of the name, the term "female Habiru" is used.

# CHAPTER 16

Observe the month of new grain, and you will sacrifice the Passover to the lord of the gods, because in the month of new grain you came out of Egypt at night. You will sacrifice the Passover to the lord of the gods, both sheep and oxen in the place which the lord of the gods will choose to have his name called. You will not eat leaven with it, seven days will you eat unleavened bread with it, the bread of affliction, because you came out of Egypt in a hurry, so you may remember the day that you came out of the land of Egypt all the days of your life. Leaven will not be seen by you in all your borders for seven days, and there will not be left any of the flesh which you will sacrifice in the evening on the first day until the next morning. You will not have power to sacrifice the Passover in any of the cities, which the lord of the gods gives you, but in the place which the lord of the gods will choose, to have his name called there, you will sacrifice the Passover at the setting of the sun, the same time when you came out of Egypt.

You will boil and roast and eat it in the place, which the lord of the gods will choose, and you will return in the morning, and go to your houses. Six days you will eat unleavened bread, and on the seventh day is a holiday, a feast to the lord of the gods. You will not do any work on it, except what must be done by a mind. Seven weeks will you count for yourself, when you have begun to put the sickle to the grain, you will begin to count seven weeks. You will keep the feast of weeks to the lord of the gods, accordingly as your hand has power in as many things as the lord of the gods will give you. You will rejoice before the lord of the gods, you and your son, and your daughter, your man-slave and your woman-slave, and the Levites, and the stranger, and the orphan, and the widow who lives among you, in whatever place the lord of the gods will choose, that his name should be called there.

You will remember that you were a servant in the land of Egypt, and you will observe and do these commands. You will keep for yourself the feast of tabernacles seven days when you gather your produce from your grain floor and your winepress. You will rejoice in your feast, you, and your son, and your daughter, your man-slave, and your woman-slave, and the Levites, and the stranger, and the orphan, and the widow that is in your cities. Seven days you will keep a feast to the lord of the gods in the place which the lord of the gods will choose for himself, and if the lord of the gods will bless you in all your fruits, and in every work of your hands, then you will rejoice. Three times in the year will all your males appear before the lord of the gods in the place which the Lord will choose in the feast of unleavened bread, and in the feast of weeks, and in the feast of tabernacles. You will not appear before the lord of the gods empty-handed. Each one according to his ability, according to the blessing of the lord of the gods which he has given you.

# CHAPTER 16

You will make for yourself judges and officers in your cities, which the lord of the gods gives you in your tribes, and they will judge the people with righteous judgment: they will not seize judgment for favor persons, nor receive gifts, because gifts blind the eyes of the wise, and pervert the words of the righteous. You will justly pursue justice, that you may live, and go in and inherit the land which the lord of the gods gives you. You will not raise for yourself an Asherah,[1] you will not plant for yourself any tree near the altar of your god. You will not set up for yourself a stele,[2] which the lord of the gods hates.

## CHAPTER 16 NOTES

**1** Codex Vaticanus: alsos (ⲁⲗⲥⲟⲥ). Translation: grove (or woods)

• Septuagint manuscript 82: assos (Λοσσς)

• Leningrad Codex: 'Ăšērâ (אֲשֵׁרָה). Translation: Asherah

• Peshitta: štltâ (ܫܬܠܬܐ). Translation: seedlings (or saplings)

• Targum Onkelos: 'Ăšērat (אֲשֵׁרַת). Translation: Asherah (or permit, license)

• Targum Pseudo-Jonathan: 'Ăšērātā' (אֲשֵׁירָתָא). Translation: Asherah (or permit, license)

• Sahidic manuscript 17: noueiehšēn (ⲛⲟⲩⲉⲓⲉ2ϣⲏⲛ). Translation: a valley of trees

• Sahidic manuscript 2006: noueiahšēn (ⲛⲟⲩⲉⲓⲁ2ϣⲏⲛ). Translation: a valley of trees

Asherah was the name of an Israelite goddess before the time of Elijah in the 9th century BCE, described as the mother of Yahweh,

# CHAPTER 16

and the wife of El. According to the books of the *Kingdoms* (Masoretic *Kings*), she was worshiped in King Solomon's Temple along with a Ba'al, presumably Ba'al Shalim, who Jerusalem and Solomon was named after. Like Atum, the Egyptian version of Shalim, the god's wife was associated with the night sky and worshiped by planting a sacred tree, and known as the title 'Hand of god.' In the case of Asherah, her sacred tree was the oak tree, which is a self-pollinating "virgin" tree. Important Canaanite graves were marked by planting oak acorns, which grew into "living tombstones." As the Greek term alsos was a translation of Asherah, the name is restored from the Leningrad Codex.

**2** Codex Vaticanus: stēlēn (ϹΤΗΛΗΝ). Translation: stele (or column, pile, pillar)

• Leningrad Codex: maṣṣēbâ (מַצֵּבָה). Translation: gravestone

• Peshitta: qymtå (ܩܝܡܬܐ). Translation: tombstone (or tree stump, resurrection)

• Targum Onkelos: qāmā' (קָמָא). Translation: pillar (or statue)

• Targum Pseudo-Jonathan: qāmā' (קָמָא). Translation: pillar (or statue)

• Sahidic manuscript 17: ouoeit (ⲞⲨⲞⲈⲓⲦ). Translation: pillar (or stele)

# CHAPTER 17

You will not sacrifice to the lord of the gods a calf or a sheep, in which there is an imperfection, or any evil thing, for it is an abomination to the lord of the gods. If there should be found in any one of your cities, which the lord of the gods gives you, a man or a woman who will do that which is evil before the lord of the gods, to transgress his covenant, and they should go to serve and worship other gods, Shemesh,[1] Yarikh,[2] any of those from the worlds of the sky which I do not command.[3] If it is reported to you, and you have inquired diligently, and, know the thing really took place, and this abomination has been done in Israel, then you will bring out that man or woman, and you will stone them with stones, and they will die. He will die on the testimony of two or three witnesses, a man who is put to death will not be put to death according to one witness. The hand of the witnesses will be among the first to put him to death, and the hands of the other people will follow, and so will you remove the evil one from among yourselves.

If a matter will be too hard for you to judge, blood between blood, cause between cause, stroke between stroke, and contradiction between contradiction, or other matters of judgment in your cities, then you will rise and go up to the place which the lord of the gods will choose, and you will come to the priests the Levites, and to the judge who will exist in those days, and they will study the matter and report the judgment to you. You will act according to the things which they will report to you out of the place which the lord of the gods will choose, and you will observe all that has been commanded in the law. You will do according to the law and to the judgment which they will declare to you. You will not swerve to the right hand or the left from any sentence which they will report to you.

The man that will act in haughtiness, and not listen to the priest who stands to minister in the name of the lord of the gods, or the judge who will preside in those days, that man will die, and you will remove the evil one out of Israel. All the people will hear and fear, and will no longer lack reverence.

When you enter into the land which the lord of the gods gives you, and will inherit it and live in it, and will say, "I will set a king[4] over me, as also the other nations around me." You will certainly set over you the king who the lord of the gods will choose, from your brothers you will set a king over you. You will not set over you a stranger who is not your brother. He will not multiply for himself horses, and he will not return the people to Egypt. If he should multiply for himself horses, for the Lord said, "You will not anymore return that way."

He will not multiply for himself wives, in case his heart changes, and he will not greatly multiply for himself silver and gold. When he has been established in his government, then he will copy for himself the law into a book by the hands of the priests the Levites, and it will be with him, and

# CHAPTER 17

he will read it all the days of his life, that he may learn to fear the lord of the gods, and keep all these commandments, and to observe these ordinances so that his heart does not become elevated from his brothers, and so that he doesn't depart from the commandments on the right hand or the left. Then he and his sons may reign long in his dominion among the children of Israel.

## CHAPTER 17 NOTES

**1** Codex Vaticanus: ēliō (ＨＡＩＣＯ). Translation Helios (or sun)

- Leningrad Codex: šemeš (שֶׁמֶשׁ). Translation: Shemesh (or sun)

- Peshitta: šmšå (ܫܡܫܐ). Translation: sun

- Targum Onkelos: šimšā' (שִׁמְשָׁא). Translation: sun

- Targum Pseudo-Jonathan: šimšā' (שִׁמְשָׁא). Translation: sun

- Sahidic manuscript 17: Rē (ＰＨ). Translation: Ra (or sun)

Shemesh (ᗯᎮᗯ) was the Canaanite god of the sun, the equivalent of the Akkadian Shamshu (𒀭), Greek Helios (Ηλιω), and Egyptian Ra (𓇳𓏤𓀭). By the era of King Josiah, the sun gods were dominant throughout the region, with the Babylonians worshiping <sup>deity</sup>Marduk (𒀭𒀫𒌓) the "sun/calf god" as the supreme God, and the Egyptians worshiping Amen (𓇋𓏠𓈖𓀭) as the sun god, father god in the Theban trinity, and supreme God of Egypt. Based on 1<sup>st</sup> Ezra, after the king of Egypt killed King Josiah, he restored the worship of the "Lord," which had to have been either Shemesh or Shalim, as Egyptian records report he was a worshiper Ra, Amen, and Atum, the Egyptian sun gods.

**2** Codex Vaticanus: Selēnē (ⲥⲉⲗⲏⲛⲏ). Translation: Selene (or moon)

- Leningrad Codex: Yārēaḥ (יָרֵחַ). Translation: Yarikh (or moon)

- Peshitta: shrå (ܣܗܪܐ). Translation: crescent (or moon, silver)

- Targum Onkelos: sîhărā' (סִיהֲרָא). Translation: crescent (or moon, silver)

- Targum Pseudo-Jonathan: sîhărā' (סִיהֲרָא). Translation: crescent (or moon, silver)

- Sahidic manuscript 17: ooh (ⲟⲟϩ). Translation: moon

Yrǩ / Yrh (𐤉𐤓𐤊 / 𐤉𐤓𐤇) was the Canaanite god of the moon, the equivalent of the Sabaen Wrǩ (𐩥𐩧𐩫), Aramaic Yrhå (𐡉𐡓𐡇𐡀), Sumerian ᵈᵉⁱᵗʸNanna (𒀭𒋀𒆠), Akkadian Sin (𒂗𒍪), North Egyptian Îôḥw (𓇹𓐰𓏤𓅱), South Egyptian Ǩnsw (𓐍𓈖𓋴𓅱), and Greek Selene (Σελήνη).

The moon god may have been dominant in Southern Canaan and Hejaz Mountains, which the Neo-Babylonian king Nabonidus believed, however, that would have been long before the era of Josiah. The city of Jericho appears to have been named after the Canaanite moon god Yrh, and was one of the major fortified cities in the region for thousands of years before it was destroyed around 1500 BCE. Nabonidus attempted to restore the worship of the moon god briefly, however, lost his empire to the Persians.

**3** Codex Vaticanus: panti tōn ek tou kosmou tou $\overline{OUNOU}$ a ou prosetaxen (ⲡⲁⲛⲧⲓ ⲧⲱⲛ ⲉⲕ ⲧⲟⲩ ⲕⲟⲥⲙⲟⲩ ⲧⲟⲩ $\overline{ⲟⲩⲛⲟⲩ}$ ⲁ ⲟⲩ ⲡⲣⲟⲥⲉⲧⲁⲝⲉⲛ). Translation: any (or all, each) those from (or out, of) the cosmos (or worlds, universe) the vaulted-sky (or Uranus) which not command

- Codex Alexandrinus: panti tōn kosmō tō ek ouranou a ou prosetaxa (ⲡⲁⲛⲧⲓ ⲧⲱⲛ ⲕⲟⲥⲙⲱ ⲧⲱ ⲉⲕ ⲟⲩⲣⲁⲛⲟⲩ ⲁ ⲟⲩ ⲡⲣⲟⲥⲉⲧⲁⲝⲁ). Translation: any (or all, each) the cosmos (or worlds, universe) those from the vaulted-sky (or Uranus) which not command

• Codex Venetus: panti tōn kosmou tō ek ouranou a ou proetaxa soi (ΠΑΝΤΙ ΤѠΝ ΚΌϹΜΟΥ ΤѠ ΕΚ ΟΥΡΑΝΟΥ Α ΟΥ ΠΡΟΕΤΑΖΑ ϹΟΙ). Translation: any (or all, each) the cosmos (or worlds, universe) those from the vaulted-sky (or Uranus) which not command you

• Septuagint manuscript 707: panti to ek tou kosmou tou ouranou a ou prosetaxa (πᾰῄͥ το ϭιͨ τѡ κϙϭμου τѡ ουϱανου ᾱ ου πϙοϭτᾱζᾱ). Translation: any (or all, each) those from (or out, of) the cosmos (or worlds, universe) the vaulted-sky (Uranus) which not command

• Septuagint manuscript 29: panti tōn en tou kosmō tou ouranou a ou prosetaxa (πᾰῄͥ τ̂ͬ͠ ͨν τѡ κϙϭμͣ τѡ ουϱανου ᾱ ου πϙοϭτᾱζᾱ). Translation: any (or all, each) those in the cosmos (or worlds, universe) of the vaulted-sky (or Uranus) which not command

• Septuagint manuscript 130: panti tōn en tou kosmou tou ouranou a ou prosetaxai (πᾰῄͥ τ̂ͬ͠ ͨν τѡ κϙϭμου τѡ ουϱανου ᾱ ου πϙοϭτᾱζᾳ). Translation: any (or all, each) those in the cosmos (or worlds, universe) of the vaulted-sky (or Uranus) which not command

• Leningrad Codex: ləkol-səbā' haŠŠāmayim 'ăšer lō'-siwwîtî (לְכׇל־צְבָא הַשָּׁמַיִם אֲשֶׁר לֹא־צִוִּיתִי). Translation: every (or all, whole) military (or army) the skies (or Shamayim) which not I ordered

• Peshitta: lkl ḥylwtå dšmyå dlå pqdt (ܠܟܠ ܚܝܠܘܬܐ ܕܫܡܝܐ ܕܠܐ ܦܩܕܬ). Translation: every (or all, whole) military (or army) of the sky which not I command

• Targum Onkelos: ləkol hêlê šəmayyā' dî lā' paqqēdît (לְכׇל חֵילֵי שְׁמַיָּא דִּי לָא פַקֵּדִית). Translation: every (or all, whole) army (or valor) of the sky which not I command

• Targum Pseudo-Jonathan: ləkol hêlā' šəmayā' dəlā' paqqêdît (לְכׇל חֵילָא שְׁמַיָּא דְּלָא פַקֵּידִית). Translation: every (or all, whole) army (or valor) of the sky which not I command

# CHAPTER 17

As the Greek and Hebrew texts do not correlate, the Greek text is followed.

**4** Codex Alexandrinus: arǩontas (ⲀⲢⲬⲞⲚⲦⲀⲤ). Translation: king (or ruler)

- Septuagint manuscript 848: arǩonta (αρχ℗τλ). Translation: king (or ruler)
- Leningrad Codex: melek (מֶ֫לֶךְ). Translation: king
- Peshitta: mlkå (ܡܠܟܐ). Translation: king
- Targum Onkelos: malkā' (מַלְכָּא). Translation: king
- Targum Pseudo-Jonathan: malkā' (מַלְכָּא). Translation: king
- Sahidic manuscript 17: arǩōn (ⲀⲢⲬⲰⲚ). Translation: king

# CHAPTER 18

The priests, the Levites, including the whole tribe of Levi, have no part nor inheritance with Israel. The burnt offerings of the Lord are their inheritance, and they will eat them. They have no inheritance among their brothers. The Lord himself has his portion as he said. This is the due of the priests in the things coming from the people from those who offer sacrifices, whether it be a calf or a sheep, and you will give the shoulder to the priest, and the cheeks, and the great intestine, and the first fruits of your grain, and of your wine, and of your oil, and you will give to him the first fruits of the fleeces of your sheep.

The Lord has chosen them out of all your tribes, to stand before the lord of the gods, to minister and bless in his name, himself, and his sons among the children of Israel. If a Levite comes from one of the cities of all the children of Israel, where he lives, accordingly as his own desires, to the place which he has chosen, he will minister in the name of Lord his god, as all his brothers the Levites, who stand there present before the lord of the gods. He will eat an allotted portion, besides the sale of his hereditary property.

When you have entered into the land which the lord of the gods gives you, you will not learn to do according to the abominations of those nations. There will not be found among you one who purges his son or his daughter with fire, one who divines, who deals with omens, and augury, a sorcerer employing incantation, one who has in him a divining spirit, and observer of signs, questioning the dead. For everyone that does these things is an abomination to the lord of the gods, because all of these abominations the Lord will destroy them from in front of you. You will be perfect before the lord of the gods. For all these nations whose land you will inherit, they listen to omens and divination, which the lord of the gods has not permitted you to do. The lord the gods will raise for you a prophet from your brothers, like me. You will listen to him, according to all things which you did desire of the lord of the gods in Horeb in the day of the assembly, saying, "We will not hear again the voice of the lord of the gods, and we will not anymore see this great fire, and so we will not die."

The Lord said to me, "They have spoken rightly, all that they have said to you. I will raise for them a prophet from their brothers, like you. I will put my words in his mouth, and he will speak them as I command him. Whatever man will not listen to whatever words that prophet says in my name, I will take vengeance on him. But the prophet whoever will impiously speak in my name a word which I have not commanded him to speak, and whoever will speak in the name of other gods, that prophet will die. But if you will say in your heart, 'How will we know which words the Lord has not spoken?' Whatever words that prophet will speak in the name of the Lord, and they will not come true, and not come to pass, this is the thing which the Lord has not spoken. That prophet has spoken wickedly. You will not spare him."

# CHAPTER 19

When the lord of the gods has destroyed the nations which God gives you, all the land, and you will inherit them, and live in their cities, and in their houses, you will separate for yourself three cities among your land, which the lord of the gods gives you. Take a survey of your way, and you will divide the coasts of your land, which the lord of the gods apportions to you, into three parts, and there will be there a refuge for every murderer. This will be the ordinance of the murderer, who will flee there, and will live, whoever has killed his neighbor ignorantly and he didn't hate him previously. Whoever will enter in the woods with his neighbor, to gather wood, and if the hand of him cutting wood with the ax should be violently shaken, and the ax-head falls off from the handle and should land on his neighbor, and he should die, he will flee to one of these cities to live.

In case the avenger of blood chases after the slayer because his heart is hot, and catches him because the way is too long, and slays him, even though there is on this man no sentence of death because he didn't hate him previously. Therefore I order you, "You will separate for yourself three cities. If the Lord will enlarge your borders, as he swore to your fathers, and the Lord will give you all the land which he said he would give to your fathers, if you will listen to do all these commands, which I order you today, to love the lord of the gods, and to follow all his ways continually, you will add for yourself yet three cities to these three. So innocent blood will not be spilled in the land, which the lord of the gods gives you to inherit, and there will not be in you one guilty of blood." But if there should be among you a man, hating his neighbor, and he should lay in wait for him, and rise up against him, and kill him so that he dies, and he should flee to one of these cities, then the elders of his city will send, and take him from there and they will deliver him into the hands of the avengers of blood, and he will die. Your eye will not spare him, and you will purge the innocent blood from Israel, and it will go well with you.

You will not move the landmarks of your neighbor, which your fathers set in the inheritance, in which you have obtained a share in the land, which the lord of the gods gives you to inherit. One witness will not stand to testify against a man for any iniquity, or for any fault, or for any sin which he may commit, by the mouth of two witnesses, or by the mouth of three witnesses, will every ruling be established. If an unjust witness rises against a man, alleging iniquity against him, then will the two men between whom the controversy is, stand before the Lord, and before the priests, and before the judges, who may exist in those days. The judges will make a diligent investigation, if an unjust witness has given false testimony, and has stood against his brother, then you will do to him as he wickedly devised to do against his brother, and you will remove the evil from yourselves. The rest will hear and fear and do no more of this evil among you. Your eye will not spare him. You will exact life for life, eye for an eye, tooth for tooth, hand for hand, and foot for foot.

# CHAPTER 20

If you should go out to war against your enemies and should see cavalry, and a more numerous people than yourself, you will not be afraid of them, for the lord of the gods is with you, who brought you up out of the land of Egypt. It will come to pass whenever you will come close to battle that the priest will come close and speak to the people and will say to them, "Listen Israel, you are going this day to battle against your enemies. Don't let your heart faint, don't be afraid, nor be confused, nor turn aside from their face. For it is the lord of the gods who advances with you, to fight with you against your enemies, and to save you."

The scribes will say to the people, "What man is he that has built a new house, and has not dedicated it? Let him go and return to his house, in case he dies in the war, and another man dedicates it. What man has planted a vineyard, and not been made happy with it? Let him go and return to his house, in case he dies in the battle, and another man be made happy with it. What man is betrothed a wife, and has not taken her? Let him go and return to his house, in case he dies in the battle, and another man takes her."

The scribes will speak further to the people, and say, "What man fears and is cowardly in his heart? Let him go and return to his house, in case he makes the heart of his brother fail, like his own." It will come to pass when the scribes have ceased speaking to the people, that they will appoint generals of the army to be leaders of the people. If you will come close to a city to conquer them by war, then call them out peaceably. If then they should answer peaceably to you, and open to you, it will be that all the people found in it will be tributary and slaves to you. But if they will not listen to you, but wage war against you, you will besiege it, until the lord of the gods delivers it into your hands, and you will kill every male from it with the edge of the sword, except the women and the stock, and all the livestock, and whatever will be in the city, and all the plunder you will take as spoil for yourself, and will eat all the plunder of your enemies whom the lord of the gods gives you.

This you will do to all the cities that are very far away from you, not being of the cities of these nations which the lord of the gods gives you to inherit. Of these you will not take anything alive; but you will certainly curse them, the Cypriots, and the Amorites, and the Canaanites, and the Perizzites, and the Mitanni, and the Jebusites, and the Girgashites, as the lord of the gods commanded you. That they may not teach you to do all their abominations, which they did for their gods, and so you should sin before the lord of the gods. If you should besiege a city many days to prevail against it by war to take it, you will not destroy its trees, by applying an iron tool to them, but you will eat of it, and will not cut it down. Is the tree that is in the field a man, to enter against you into the work of the siege? But the tree which you know to not be fruit-bearing, this you will destroy and cut down, and you will construct a mound against the city, which makes war against you until it is delivered up.

# CHAPTER 21

If one is found slain with the sword in the land, which the lord of the gods gives you to inherit, having fallen in the field, and they do not know who has killed him, your elders and your judges will come out and will measure the distances of the cities around the slain man. It will be that the city which is nearest to the slain man the elders of that city will take a heifer from the herd, which has not labored, and which has not pulled a yoke.

The elders of that city will bring down the heifer to a rough valley, which has not been tilled and is not sown, and they will cut the sinews of the heifer in the valley. The priests, the Levites, will come because the lord of the gods has chosen them to stand by him, and to bless in his name, and by their word will every controversy and every stroke be decided. All the elders of that city who come close to the slain man will wash their hands over the head of the heifer which was slain in the valley, and they will answer and say, "Our hands have not shed this blood, and our eyes have not seen it. Be merciful to your people Israel, whom you have redeemed, Lord, that innocent blood may not be on your people Israel," and the blood will be atoned for by them. You will take away the innocent blood from among you if you should do that which is good and pleasing before the lord of the gods.

If when you go out to war against your enemies, the lord of the gods should deliver them into your hands, and you should take their spoil, and should see among the spoil a woman beautiful in appearance, and should think about her, and take her for yourself for a wife, and should bring her within your house, then you will shave her head, and pare her nails, and will take away her garments of captivity from off her, and she will live in your house and will mourn her father and mother for a month, and afterward, you will go into her and live with her, and she will be your wife. If you do not delight in her, you will send her away free, and she will not by any means be sold for silver, you will not treat her contemptuously, because you have humbled her.

If a man has two wives, the one loved and the other hated, and both the loved and the hated should have born him children, and the son of the hated should be firstborn, then it will be that whenever he will divide by inheritance his goods to his sons, he will not be able to give the right of the firstborn to the son of the loved one, having ignored the son of the hated, which is the firstborn. But he will acknowledge the firstborn of the hated one and give to him double of all things which will be found by him, because he is the beginning of his children, and to him belongs the birthright.

If any man has a disobedient and contentious son, who does not listen to the voice of his father and the voice of his mother, and they should correct him, and he should not listen to them, then his father and his mother will take hold of him and bring him to the elders of his city, and the gate of the place and they will say to the men of their city, "Our son is disobedient and contentious, and he does not listen to our voice. He is a reveler and a drunkard." The men of his city will stone him with stones, and he will die. You will remove the evil one from yourselves, and the rest will hear and fear.

If there is sin in anyone, and the judgment of death be on him, and he is put to death, and you hang him in a tree, his body will not remain all night on the tree, but you will, by all means, bury it in that day, for everyone that is hanged in a tree is cursed by God, and you will by no means defile the land which the lord of the gods gives you for an inheritance.

# CHAPTER 22

When you see the calf of your brother or his sheep wandering in the road, you will not ignore them, you will, by all means, return them to your brother, and you will restore them to him. If your brother does not come to you, and you do not know him, you will bring it into your house within, and it will be with you until your brother will seek them, and you will restore them to him. This you will do with his donkey, and you this will do to his garment, and this you will do to everything that your brother has lost, whatever has been lost by him, and you have found, which you will not ignore.

You will not see the donkey of your brother, or his calf, fallen on the road. You will not ignore them, you will certainly help raise them.

The clothing of a man will not be worn by a woman, neither will a man put on a woman's dress, for everyone that does these things is an abomination to the lord of the gods.

If you should come across a nest of birds in front of you along the road, or in a tree, or on the ground, young or eggs and the mother who is brooding on the young or the eggs, you will not take the mother with the young ones. You will let the mother go, but you will take the young for yourself, that it may go well with you, and that you may live long.

# CHAPTER 22

If you should build a new house, then you will make a parapet to your house, so you will not bring blood-guiltiness to your house if one should in any way fall from it.

You will not sow your vineyard with diverse seeds, in case the fruit is devoted to whatever seed you may sow with the fruit of your vineyard.

You will not plow with an ox and a donkey together.

You will not wear a false garment, wool, and linen together. You will make fringes on the four borders of your garments, with whatever you may be clothed.

If anyone should take a wife, and live with her, and hate her, and use terrible words against her, and bring against her an evil name, and say, "I took this woman, and when I came to her I found in her no tokens of virginity," then the father and the mother of the girl will take and bring out the girl's tokens of virginity to the elders of the city to the gate.

The father of the girl will say to the elders, "I gave my daughter to this man as a wife, and now he hates her, and uses terrible words against her, saying, 'I have not found tokens of virginity with your daughter.' Yet these are the tokens of my daughter's virginity." They will unfold the garment before the elders of the city. The elders of that city will take that man, and will chastise him, and will fine him a hundred shekels, and will give them to the father of the girl, because he has brought out an evil name against a virgin of Israel, and she will be his wife. He will never be able to divorce her. But if this report is true, and the tokens of virginity are not found for the girl, then will they bring out the girl to the doors of her father's house, and will stone her with stones, and she will die, because she has worked folly among the children of Israel, to defile the house of her father by whoring, and so you will remove the evil one from among you.

If a man is found sleeping with a woman married to another man, you will kill them both, the man that slept with the woman, and the woman, and so you will remove the wicked one out of Israel.

If there is a young girl married to a man, and a man found her in the city and has slept with her, you will bring them both out to the gate of their city, and they will be stoned with stones, and they will die, the girl, because she did not cry out in the city, and the man, because he humbled his neighbor's spouse, and so you will remove the evil one from yourselves. But if a man finds out in the field, a girl that is engaged and he should rape her, you will slay the man that raped her only. The girl has not committed a sin worthy of death, like when a man should rise against his neighbor, and slay him, so is this thing, because he found her in the field, and the betrothed girl cried out, and there was none to help her.

If anyone should find a young virgin who has not been engaged and should rape her, and be caught, the man who raped her will give to the father of the girl fifty silver didrachms,[1] and she will be his wife because he has humbled her. He will never be able to divorce her. A man will not take his father's wife, and will not uncover his father's skirt.

# CHAPTER 22

## CHAPTER 22 NOTES

**1** Codex Alexandrinus: pentēkonta didrakma arguriou (ΠΕΝΤΗΚΟΝΤΑ ΔΙΔΡΑΧΜΑ ΑΡΓΥΡΙΟΥ). Translation: fifty double-drachmas of silver

• Codex Ambrosiano A 147: pentēkonta didragma arguriou (ΠΕΝΤΗΚΟΝΤΑ ΔΙΔΡΑΓΜΑ ΑΡΓΥΡΙΟΥ). Translation: fifty double-drachmas of silver

• Septuagint manuscript 82: pentēkonta arguriou didrakma (πεντλu⊕τλ Αβγυβιου ΔΩεαχuα). Translation: fifty silver double-drachmas

• Leningrad Codex: ḥămiššîm kāsep (חֲמִשִּׁים כָּסֶף). Translation: fifty silvers

• Peshitta: ḥmšyn dkspå (ܫܚܡܫܝܢ ܕܟܣܦܐ). Translation: fifty of silvers

• Targum Onkelos: ḥamšîn sil'în diksap (חַמְשִׁין סִלְעִין דִּכְסָף). Translation: fifty selas of silver

• Targum Pseudo-Jonathan: ḥamšîn sal'în diksap (חַמְשִׁין סַלְעִין דִּכְסָף). Translation: fifty selas of silver

• Sahidic manuscript 17: sateere nhat (ⲥⲁⲧⲉⲉⲣⲉ ⲛ̄ϩⲁⲧ). Translation: staters of silver

The Greek translation includes the measurement of didrachma, which is missing from the Leningrad Codex. In other books of the Septuagint, the term didrachma is mirrored in the Masoretic Text by shekel, which imported into this translations as it must have been in the Aramaic source texts the Greeks used. In the later Aramaic targums, the translation of "selas" was used, however, this was a different coin and unit of measurement.

160

# CHAPTER 23

He who is damaged or mutilated in his private parts will not enter into the assembly of the Lord. One born of a harlot will not enter into the assembly of the Lord. The Ammonite and Moabite will not enter into the assembly of the Lord, even until the tenth generation he will not enter into the assembly of the Lord, even forever, because they did not meet you with bread and water along the road, when you went out of Egypt, and because they hired Balaam the son of Beor of Mesopotamia[1] to curse you. But the lord of the gods would not listen to Balaam, and the lord of the gods changed the curses into blessings because the lord of the gods loved you. You will not speak peaceably or profitably to them all your days forever.

You will not hate an Edomite, because he is your brother. You will not hate an Egyptian, because you were a stranger in his land. If sons are born to them, in the third generation they will enter into the assembly of the Lord.

If you should go out to engage with your enemies, then you will keep away from every wicked thing. If there should be among you a man who is not clean because of his issue by night, then he will go out of the camp, and he will not enter into the camp. It will come to pass toward evening he will wash his body with water, and when the sun has gone down, he will go into the camp.

# CHAPTER 23

You have a place outside of the camp, and you will go out there, and you have a trowel on your girdle, and it will come to pass when you would relieve yourself outside, that you will dig with it, and will bring back the dirt and cover your waste.

Because the lord of the gods walks in your camp to deliver you and to give up your enemy in front of you, your camp will be holy, and there will not appear among you a disgraceful thing, or he will turn away from you.

You will not return a slave to his master, who running from his master attaches himself to you. He will live with you, he will live among you where he will please. You will not punish him.

There will not be a harlot from the daughters of Israel, and there will not be a fornicator from the sons of Israel. There will not be a healer[2] among the daughters of Israel, and there will not be an initiate[3] among the sons of Israel.

You will not bring the wages of a whore,[4] or the price of a dog[5] into the Temple of the lord of the gods, for any vow because both are an abomination to the lord of the gods.

You will not lend to your brother on interest of silver, or interest of meat, or interest of anything which you may lend out. You may lend on interest to a stranger, but to your brother, you will not lend on interest, that the lord of the gods may bless you in all your works on the land, into which you are entering to inherit.

# CHAPTER 23

If you will vow a vow to the lord of the gods, you will not
delay paying it, for the lord of the gods will certainly require
it of you, and otherwise, it will be a sin for you. But if you
should be unwilling to vow, it is not a sin for you. You will
remember the words that come from between your lips, and
as you have vowed a gift to the lord of the gods, you will do
that which you have said with your mouth.

## CHAPTER 23 NOTES

**1** Codex     Vaticanus:     Mesopotamias     (ΜΕϹΟΠΟΤΑΜΙΑϹ).
Translation: Mesopotamia

• Septuagint     manuscript     376:     Mesōpotamias     (Μϛ͞ωποτΔμΔϲ).
Translation: Mesopotamia

• Septuagint     manuscript     44:     Mesopotamias     (Μϛ͞σωποτΔμϕΔϲ).
Translation: Mesopotamia

• Leningrad Codex: Pətôr 'Ăram nahărayim (פְּתוֹר אֲרַם נַהֲרַיִם).
Translation: Petor Aram rivers

• Peshitta: Pytwr dÅrm nhryn (ܦܬܘܪ ܕܐܪܡ ܢܗܪܝܢ). Translation:
Pytwr of Aram Rivers

• Targum Onkelos: Pətôr 'Ăram dî 'al pərāt (פְּתוֹר אֲרַם דִּי עַל פְּרָת).
Translation: Petor Aram that on Euphrates

• Targum Pseudo-Jonathan: Pətôr Helmayā' dəmitbanyā' bə'ara'
'Ăram də'al Pərāt (פְּתוֹר חֶלְמַיָּא דְּמִתְבַּנְיָא בְּאַרַע אֲרַם דְּעַל פְּרָת).
Translation: Petor Chelmaya (or dreamer) which is built in the land
of Aram on the Euphrates

• Sahidic     manuscript     17:     Mesopotamia ntSuria (ΜΕϹΟΠΟΤΑΜΙΑ
ΝΤϹΥΡΙΑ). Translation: Mesopotamia in Syria

# CHAPTER 23

Mesopotamia is the Greek translation of Aram-Naharayim, however, the Septuagint does not include a translation of Petor in this verse. The verses in *Numbers* that refer to Balaam, call his hometown Fatoura (Φαθουρα) in the Septuagint, and Pətôrâ (פְּתוֹרָה) in the Leningrad Codex, both of which are similar to the term used in the Leningrad Codex version of this verse.

The name of the city Pətôrâ (פְּתוֹרָה) appears to be a transliteration of the Babylonian cuneiform word Paššūru (𒑱𒂍𒊺𒈨), which meant "table." The related Aramaic word was Pāṯūrā (פְּתוֹרָא), the Syriac word was Pāṯūrā (ܦܬܘܪܐ), and the related Arabic word is fāṭūr (فَاطُور), all of which mean "table," "tray," or "platter." The older Akkadian spelling of paššūru (𒄑), which was also the spelling of the name of the city of Ur, in southern modern Iraq. If the original text of this section of text was written before the development of the Phoenician alphabet, it would have been written in Akkadian Cuneiform, the official script used in Canaan under Egyptian rule during the New Kingdom era, suggesting the transliteration error took place when the Phoenician translation was made in the early Iron Age.

**2** Codex Vaticanus: telesforos (ΤΕΛΕϹΦΟΡΟϹ). Translation: healer

• Septuagint manuscript 75: telosforos (ⲧⲉⲗⲟⲥⲫⲟⲣⲟⲥ)

• Septuagint manuscript 458: telosfōros (ⲧⲉⲗⲟⲥⲫⲟⲟⲣⲟⲥ)

• Leningrad Codex: qədēšâ (קְדֵשָׁה). Translation: holiness (or sanctify, saintliness)

• Peshitta: znytå (ܙܢܝܬܐ). Translation: fornicator

• Targum Onkelos: zannîtâ' (זַנִּיתָא). Translation: fornicator

• Targum Jerusalem: zənû (זְנוּ). Translation: fornication

• Targum Pseudo-Jonathan: tə'îtā' (טְעִיתָא). Translation: prostitute

• Sahidic manuscript 17: pornē (ⲡⲟⲣⲛⲏ). Translation: prostitute

# CHAPTER 23

This verse has been generally accepted as referring to female sacred-sex-workers, involved in sex-rites at the temples of Qetesh. There was a Palace of Qetesh reported to have been near the Temple of El in Shiloh, and another near the Temple in Jerusalem.

Various alternate theories are also suggested by researchers, including that the word simply meant Priestess of Qetesh, as the word appears to be derived from the Akkadian word "qadishu" (ⵏ⵩ⵉⵐⵙ), meaning "nun," and a separate word was used for prostitute, zônâ (זוֹנָה), which is used in the next verse. Ritualistic sex acts were documented in the Temples of Qetesh (under her various names) across the Middle East dating back to Sumerian times (before 3000 BCE), however, most recent archaeological evidence supports the idea that the prostitutes were males, transvestites, or transgender in modern parlance. Given the debate over the meaning of qədēšâ (קְדֵשָׁה), the Greek translation of healer (τελεσφόρος) is used.

**3** Codex Vaticanus: teliskomenos (ΤΕΛΙϹΚΟΜΕΝΟϹ). Translation: abstinent-initiate

• Codex Alexandrinus: teleskomenos pasan euḱēn (ΤΕΛΕϹΚΟΜΕΝΟϹ ΠΑϹΑΝ ΕΥΧΗΝ). Translation: abstinent-initiate every prayer

• Septuagint manuscript 407: teliskomenos eis pasan euḱēn (τϑιϲκομϑυος ϵϲ πλσϑυ ϑυχιω). Translation: abstinent-initiate into every prayer

• Septuagint manuscript 19: teliskomenos pros pasasan (τϑιϲκομϑυος πϱϲ πλϙϛϑυ). Translation: abstinent-initiate everyone similar

• Leningrad Codex: qādēš (קָדֵשׁ). Translation: Kadesh (or holiness)

• Peshitta: znå (ܙܢܝ). Translation: fornication

- Targum Onkelos: gabrā' mibbənê Yiśrā'ēl 'ittətā' 'āmā' (גַּבְרָא מִבְּנֵי
יִשְׂרָאֵל אִתְּתָא אָמָא). Translation: husband of the sons of Israel to a slave-woman

  - Targum Jerusalem: nəpaq bar (נְפַק בַּר). Translation: exiled son

  - Targum Pseudo-Jonathan: gabrā' bar Yiśrā'ēl yat garmêh biznû
(גַּבְרָא בַּר יִשְׂרָאֵל יַת גַּרְמֵיהּ בִּזְנוּ). Translation: husband son of Israel himself to cause through fornication (or "Israelite pimps")

- Sahidic manuscript 17: rōme šōpe (ⲣⲱⲙⲉ ϣⲱⲡⲉ). Translation: human cucumber

This verse has been generally accepted as referring to male sacred-sex-workers, involved in sex-rites at the temples of Qetesh by Christians. There was a Palace of Qetesh reported to have been near the Temple of El in Shiloh, and another near the Temple in Jerusalem.

Ritualistic sex acts were documented in the Temples of Qetesh (under her various names) across the Middle East dating back to Sumerian times (before 3000 BCE), however, most recent archaeological evidence supports the idea that the prostitutes were males, transvestites or transgender in modern parlance. These males, often eunuch, prostitutes were documented into the Roman era, however, had become rare.

While the traditional translations of "Sodomite" or "male-prostitute" may be an accurate description of the qādēš themselves, the verse does not appear to be referring to the sex-acts, but rather the group itself, and therefore the word "initiate" (τελισκόμενος) is used in this translation. Curiously, the author is not stating that the qədēšâ and qādēš should be banned, just that Israelites should not be qədēšâ and qādēš, implying it was acceptable for other nationalities to be qədēšâ and qādēš. This would date the authorship of the verse to either before King Josiah's reforms or place the authorship outside of Judah.

Alternatively, the targums that developed parallel to the Christian interpretation take several alternative viewpoints, including the statement that Israelite men could not marry slave women, not tolerate exiles, and not be pimps. Given the diversity of opinions, this translation uses the original Greek meaning of the word.

**4** Codex Vaticanus: pornēs (ΠΟΡΝΗC). Translation: whore

• Septuagint manuscript 16: pornē (πορνη)

• Leningrad Codex: zônâ (זוֹנָה). Translation: whore (or prostitute, slut, harlot)

• Dead Sea Scroll 4QDeut^g: zwnh (זונה)

• Peshitta: znytå (ܙܢܝܬܐ). Translation: fornicator

• Targum Onkelos: zannîtā' (זְנִיתָא). Translation: fornicator

• Targum Jerusalem: zənû (זְנוּ). Translation: fornication

• Targum Pseudo-Jonathan: tə'îtā' (טְעִיתָא). Translation: prostitute

• Sahidic manuscript 17: pornē (ΠΟΡΝΗ). Translation: prostitute

This verse is generally linked with the previous statement about qədēšâ and qādēš, however, uses a derogatory term for the prostitutes, implying it is a separate statement about not offering clean things to God. As the offering is silver being offered at the Temple of the Lord the god, it is clear the date of authorship is after the Israelites had settled in Canaan, and after there was both coinage and a Temple of the Lord the god, meaning after the time of King Solomon circa 950 BCE.

**5** Codex Vaticanus: kunos (ΚΥΝΟC). Translation: female dog

• Septuagint manuscript 16: koinos (κοινος). Translation: public

• Septuagint manuscript 767: koinōs (κοινως). Translation: public

• Septuagint manuscript 509: kunon (ϣ). Translation: cynic

- Septuagint manuscript 54: kuros (ⲕⲩⲣⲟⲥ). Translation: supreme power (or authority, Cyrus)
- Septuagint manuscript 72: gunaikos (ⲅⲩⲛⲁ/ⲕⲟⲥ). Translation: woman
- Leningrad Codex: keleb (כֶּלֶב). Translation: male dog
- Peshitta: klbå (ܟܠܒܐ). Translation: dog (or wild, mad, wind, Sirius)
- Targum Onkelos: kalbā' (כַּלְבָּא). Translation: dog (or wild, mad, wind, Sirius)
- Targum Jerusalem: keleb (כֶּלֶב). Translation: male dog
- Targum Pseudo-Jonathan: keleb (כֶּלֶב). Translation: male dog
- Sahidic manuscript 17: ouhor (ⲟⲩϩⲟⲣ). Translation: male dog

The term "dog" is often assumed to be related to the word "whore" earlier in the verse, and the term "initiate" in the previous verse, resulting in the mistranslation "male prostitute" in some translations, assuming the word "dog" was a slanderous term for homosexual males. The verse is simply about not offering silver acquired in unclean ways to God. Dogs were unclean animals that the Israelites kept as pets, and bought and sold, but did not eat.

# CHAPTER 24

If you should go into the grain field of your neighbor, then you may gather the ears with your hands, but you will not put the sickle to your neighbor's grain.

If you should go into the vineyard of your neighbor, you will eat grapes sufficient to satisfy your desire, but you may not put them into a vessel.

If anyone should take a wife and live with her, then it will come to pass if she should not have found favor before him, because he has found something unpleasant in her, that he will write for her a letter of divorcement, and give it to her and send her out of his house.

If she should go away and be married to another man, and the second husband should hate her, and write for her a letter of divorcement, and give it to her hands, and send her out of his house, and the second husband should die, who took her to himself as a wife, the former husband who sent her away will not be able to return and take her for himself as a wife after she has been defiled, because it is an abomination before the lord of the gods, and you will not defile the land, which the lord of the gods gives you to inherit.

If anyone should have recently taken a wife, he will not go out to war, neither will anything be laid on him, he will be guiltless in his house for one year, he will celebrate his wife whom he has taken.

# Chapter 24

You will not take for a pledge the under millstone, nor the upper millstone, for this man who does so takes life for a pledge.

If a man should be caught kidnapping a child of Israel, and having captured him he should sell him, that thief will die, and so will you remove that evil one from yourselves.

Pay attention to yourself in regarding the plague of leprosy. You will pay great attention to do according to all the laws, which the priests, the Levites will report to you. Pay attention to do, as I have ordered you. Remember all that the lord of the gods did to Mariam along the road, when you were going out of Egypt.

If your neighbor owes you a debt, any debt whatever, you will not go into his house to take his pledge. You will stand outside, and the man who is in your debt will bring the pledge out to you. If the man is poor, you will not keep his pledge overnight. You will certainly restore his pledge at sunset, and he will sleep in his garment, and he will bless you, and it will be mercy shown by you before the lord of the gods.

You will not unjustly withhold the wages of the poor and needy of your brothers, or of the strangers who are in your cities. You will pay him his wages the same day, the sun will not go down on it, because he is poor and he trusts in it, and he will cry against you to the Lord, and it will be sin in you.

# CHAPTER 24

The fathers will not be put to death for the children, and the sons will not be put to death for the fathers. Everyone will die for his own sin.

You will not wrest the judgment of the stranger and the fatherless, and widow. You will not take the widow's garment for a pledge.

You will remember that you were a slave in the land of Egypt, and the lord of the gods redeemed you from there, therefore I order you to do this thing. When you have reaped grain in your field, and have forgotten a sheaf in your field, you will not return to take it. It will be for the stranger, and the orphan and the widow, that the lord of the gods may bless you in all the works of your hands.

If you should gather your olives, you will not return to collect the remainder, it will be for the stranger, and the fatherless, and the widow, and you will remember that you were a slave in the land of Egypt, therefore I command you to do this thing.

Whenever you gather the grapes of your vineyard, you will not glean what you have left, it will be for the stranger, and the orphan, and the widow, and you will remember that you were a slave in the land of Egypt, therefore I command you to do this thing.

# CHAPTER 25

If there should be a dispute between men, and they should come forward for judgment, and the judges judge, and justify the righteous, and condemn the wicked, then it will come to pass, if the unrighteous should be worthy of stripes, you will lay him down before the judges, and they will whip him before them according to his iniquity. They will whip him with forty lashes, they will not inflict more, for if you should whip him with more lashes beyond these, your brother will be disgraced before you.

You will not muzzle the ox that treads out the grain.

If brothers should live together, and one of them should die, and should not have a child, the wife of the deceased will not marry out of the family to a man not related. Her husband's brother will go into her and will take her for himself as a wife, and will live with her. It will come to pass that the child which she will bear, will be constituted by the name of the deceased, and his name will not be blotted out of Israel.

If the man should not be willing to take his brother's wife, then the will woman go up to the gate to the elders, and she will say, "My husband's brother will not raise up the name of his brother in Israel. My husband's brother has not been willing." The elders of his city will call him, and speak to him, and if he stands and says, "I will not take her," then his brother's wife will come forward before the elders, and will remove one shoe from off his foot, and will spit in his face, and will answer and say, "This will they do to the man who will not build his brother's house in Israel." His name will be called in Israel, "The house of him that has had his shoe removed."

If men should fight, a man with his brother and the wife of one of them should approach to rescue her husband out of the hand of he that kills him, and she should stretch out her hand, and take hold of his private parts, you will cut off her hand. Your eye will not spare her.

You will not have in your bag diverse weights, a great and a small. You will not have in your house diverse measures, a great and a small. You have a true and just weight, and a true and just measure, that you may live long on the land which the lord of the gods gives you for an inheritance. For everyone that does this is an abomination to the lord of the gods, everyone that does injustice.

Remember what Amalek did to you along the road, when you left from the land of Egypt, how he blocked your way and attacked your backs, even those that were weary behind you, and you did hunger and were weary, and he did not fear god. It will come to pass whenever the lord of the gods has given you rest from all your enemies around you, in the land which the lord of the gods gives you to inherit, you will blot out the name of Amalek from under the sky, and will not forget to do it.

# CHAPTER 26

When you have entered into the land, which the lord of the gods gives you to inherit, and you have inherited it, and you have lived in it, you will take the first of the fruits of your land, which the lord of the gods gives you, and you will put them into a basket, and you will go to the place which the lord of the gods will choose to have his name called there. You will come to the priest who will exist in those days, and you will say to him, "I testify today by the lord of the gods, that I have come into the land which the Lord swore to our fathers to give to us."

The priest will take the basket out of your hands, and will set it before the altar of the lord of the gods, and he will answer and say before the lord of the gods, "My father abandoned Syria, and went down into Egypt, and stayed there with a small number, and became there a mighty nation and a great multitude. The Egyptians punished us, and humbled us, and imposed hard tasks on us. We cried out to our lord of the gods, and the Lord heard our voice and saw our humiliation, and our labor, and our affliction. The Lord brought us out of Egypt himself with his great strength, and his mighty hand, and his high arm, and with great visions, and with signs, and with wonders. He brought us into this place and gave us this land, a land flowing with milk and honey. Now, Look, I have brought the first of the fruits of the land, which you gave me, Lord, a land flowing with milk and honey."

## Chapter 26

You will leave it before the lord of the gods, and you will worship before the lord of the gods, and you will rejoice in all the good things, which the lord of the gods has given you, you and your family, and the Levites, and the aliens that are among you.

When you have completed all the tithings of your fruits in the third year, you will give the second tenth to the Levites, and stranger, and fatherless, and widow, and they will eat it in your cities, and be merry. You will say before the lord of the gods, "I have fully collected the holy things out of my house, and I have given them to the Levites, and the stranger, and the orphan, and the widow, according to all commands which you did command me: I did not transgress your command, and I did not forget it. In my distress I did not eat of them, I have not gathered of them for an unclean person, I have not given them to the dead. I have listened to the voice of our lord of the gods, I have done as you have commanded me. Look down from your sacred temple in the sky,[1] and bless your people Israel, and the land which you have given them, as you did swear to our fathers, to give to us a land flowing with milk and honey."

On this day the Lord, your god ordered you to keep all the ordinances and judgments, and you will observe and do them, with all your heart, and with all your mind. You have chosen a god today to be your god, and to follow all his ways, and to observe his ordinances and judgments, and to listen to his voice. The Lord has chosen you this day that you should be to him a unique people, as he said, to keep his commands, and that you should be above all nations, as he has made you renowned, and a pride, and glorious, that you should be a holy people to the lord of the gods, as he has spoken.

## CHAPTER 26 NOTES

**1** Codex Vaticanus: oikou tou agiou sou ek tou OUNOU (ΟΙΚΟΥ ΤΟΥ ΑΓΙΟΥ ϹΟΥ ΕΚ ΤΟΥ ΟΥΝΟΥ). Translation: temple the sacred (or saint, holy) yours from the sky (or Uranus)

• Septuagint manuscript 376: oikou so agiou sou ek tou ouranou (Θκου σο Αγιου σου ϵκ τω ουϱανου). Translation: temple yours sacred yours from the sky

• Septuagint manuscript 664: oikou sou tou agiou sou (Θκου σου τω Αγιου σου). Translation: temple of yours the sacred of yours

• Leningrad Codex: mimmə'ôn qodšəkā min-haššāmayim (מִמְּעֹ֤ון קָדְשְׁךָ֙ מִן־הַשָּׁמַ֔יִם). Translation: from abode (or home, temple) holiness (sacred, Qetesh), from the skies (or Shamayim)

• Peshitta: dqwdšk mn šmyå (ܕܩܘܕܫܟ ܡܢ ܫܡܝܐ). Translation: of holiness (or sanctity, shrine, temple) from sky

• Targum Onkelos: mimmədôr qodšāk min šəmayyā' (מִמְּדֹור קֻדְשָׁךְ מִן שְׁמַיָּא). Translation: from your circle (or circuit, dwelling) sacred in the sky

• Targum Jerusalem: mimdôr bêt šəkînat yəqārāk wəqûdəšāk min šəmayā' (מִמְּדֹור בֵּית שְׁכִינַת יְקָרָךְ וְקוּדְשָׁךְ מִן שְׁמַיָּא). Translation: from your circle (or circuit, dwelling) house (or temple, abode) where you live (or shechinah) honored (or heavy, precious, cold) and sanctified (or holy) from sky

- Targum Pseudo-Jonathan: mimdôr bêt šəkînat qûdəšāk min šəmayā' (מִמְדוֹר בֵּית שְׁכִינַת קוּדְשָׁךְ מִן שְׁמַיָא). Translation: from your circle (or circuit, dwelling) house (or temple, abode) where you live (or shechinah) sanctified (or holy) from sky

- Sahidic manuscript 2006: hi etouaab ebol hn tpe (ϩⲓ ⲉⲧⲟⲩⲁⲁⲃ ⲉⲃⲟⲗ ϩⲛ ⲧⲡⲉ). Translation: house or holy (or pure) out in the sky

# CHAPTER 27

Moses and the elders of Israel commanded, "Keep all these commands, all that I command you today. It will come to pass in the day when you will cross over the Jordan into the land which the lord of the gods gives you, that you will set up for yourself great stones, and will plaster them with plaster. You will write on these stones all the words of this law, as soon as you have crossed Jordan, when you have entered into the land, which the lord of the gods of your fathers gives you, a land flowing with milk and honey, as the lord of the gods of your fathers said to you. It will be as soon as you are gone over the Jordan, you will set up these stones, which I command you today, on Mount Ebal, and you will plaster them with plaster."

"You will build there an altar to the lord of the gods, an altar of stones, and you will not use iron on it. You will build an altar to the lord of the gods from whole stones, and you will offer on it whole burnt offerings to the lord of the gods. You will offer a peace-offering there, and you will eat and be filled, and rejoice before the lord of the gods. You will write on the stones all this law very plainly."

Moses and the priests the Levites said to all Israel, "Be silent and listen Israel, today you have become the people of the lord of the gods. You will listen to the voice of the lord of the gods and will do all his commands, and his ordinances, as many as I command you today."

# CHAPTER 27

Moses ordered the people on that day, "These will stand to bless the people on mount Gerizim having gone over the Jordan: Simeon, Levi, Judas, Issachar, Joseph, and Benjamin. These will stand for cursing on mount Ebal: Reuben, Gad, Asher, Zebulun, Dan, and Naphtali."

The Levites will answer and say to all Israel with a loud voice, "Cursed is the man whoever will make a carved or molten image, an abomination to the Lord, the work of the hands of craftsmen, and will put it in a secret place, and all the people will love Amen."[1]

"Cursed is the man that dishonors his father or his mother," and all the people will praise Amen.

"Cursed is he that removes his neighbor's landmarks," and all the people will praise Amen.

"Cursed is he that makes the blind to wander in the road," and all the people will praise Amen.

"Cursed is everyone that will pervert the judgment of the stranger, and orphan, and widow," and all the people will praise Amen.

"Cursed is he that lies with his father's wife, because he has uncovered his father's skirt," and all the people will praise Amen.

"Cursed is he that lies with any animal," and all the people will praise Amen.

"Cursed is he that lies with his sister by his father or his mother," and all the people will praise Amen.

# CHAPTER 27

"Cursed is he that lies with his daughter-in-law," and all the people will praise Amen.

"Cursed is he that lies with his wife's sister," and all the people will praise Amen.

"Cursed is he that kills his neighbor secretly," and all the people will praise Amen.

"Cursed is he whoever has taken payment to take the life of an innocent man," and all the people will praise Amen.

"Cursed is every man that continues not in all the words of this law to do them," and all the people will praise Amen.

## CHAPTER 27 NOTES

**1** Codex Vaticanus: apokriteis o laos erousin Genoito (ⲀⲦⲞⲔⲢⲒⲐⲈⲒⲤ Ⲟ ⲖⲖⲞⲤ ⲈⲢⲞⲨⲤⲒⲚ ⲄⲈⲚⲞⲒⲦⲞ). Translation: reply (or judge) the people will love (or praise) Genoito

• Codex Alexandrinus: apokriteis pas o laos erei Genoito (Ἀπολρίθ6ιc πλc ο λλοc 6ρ6ι γ6νοιτο). Translation: reply (or judge) the people will love (or praise) Genoito

• Septuagint manuscript 44: apokriteis erousin Genoito pas o laos (Ἀπολρίθc ῥουσιν ρα⊕το πλc ο λλοc). Translation: to choose (or to judge) love (or praise) Genoito all the people

• Septuagint manuscript 75: apokritentes pas o laos erousin Genoito (Ἀπολρίθωτ6c πλc ο λλοc ῥουσιν ρα⊕το). Translation: set apart (or separate) all the people will love (or praise) Genoito

# CHAPTER 27

• Septuagint manuscript 376: apocritentes pas o laos oti Genoito (Ἀπουβριθὴς πᾶς ο λαος ὄμ Γαιθτο). Translation: set apart (or separate) all the people will love (or praise) Genoito

• Leningrad Codex: 'ānû kol-hā'ām wə'āmərû 'āmēn (עָנוּ כָל־הָעָם וְאָמְרוּ אָמֵן). Translation: reply (or answer) all the nation will say (or see, witness in Akkadian) Amen

• Shapira scrolls: wȯnw kl hȯm wȧmrw ȧmn (𐤅𐤏𐤍𐤅 𐤊𐤋 𐤄𐤌 𐤅𐤀𐤌𐤓𐤅 𐤀𐤌𐤍). Translation: and humble all the nation and pronounce Amen

• Peshitta: nȯnwn klh ȯmȧ wnȧmrwn ȧmyn (ܥܢܘ ܟܠܗ ܥܡܐ ܘܢܐܡܪܘܢ ܐܡܝܢ). Translation: answeredall the nation and will command (or Aries, lamb) Amen

• Targum Onkelos: wîtîbûn kol 'ammā' wəyêmərûn 'āmēn (וְיִתִיבוּן כָּל עַמָּא וְיֵימְרוּן אָמֵן). Translation: returned all the people and said Amen

• Targum Jerusalem: wə'îlên wə'āmərîn 'āmēn (וְאִילֵין וְאָמְרִין אָמֵן). Translation: and those and said Amen

• Targum Pseudo-Jonathan: wəšawê bətûmərā' hăwôn 'anyayn kûləhôn kahădā' wə'āmərîn 'āmēn (וְשַׁוֵּי בְטוּמְרָא הֲווֹן עַנְיַין כּוּלְהוֹן כַּחֲדָא וְאָמְרִין אָמֵן). Translation: and leavinga secret hiding place producing (or residing, falling) poverty (or delayed) all rejoiced and said Amen

• Sahidic manuscript 2006: ereplaos ouōšb nfjoos je efešōpe (ⲉⲣⲉⲡⲗⲁⲟⲥ ⲟⲩⲱϣⲃ ⲛϥϫⲟⲟⲥ ϫⲉ ⲉϥⲉϣⲱⲡⲉ). Translation: if the people respond (or answer) and will say "become"

The Greek translation is quite different from the Hebrew, suggesting the Aramaic was different. Genoito (Γενοιτο) was a Greek expression, meaning "Earth forbid," which was used as a translation of "amen."

# CHAPTER 28

It will come to pass, if you will indeed hear the voice of the lord of the gods, to observe and do all these commands, which I order you this day, that the lord of the gods will set you on high above all the nations of the earth, and all these blessings will come on you and will find you. If you will indeed hear the voice of the lord of the gods, blessed you will be in the city, and blessed you will be in the field. Blessed will be the offspring of your belly, and the fruits of your land, and your oxen herds, and your sheep flocks. Blessed will be your barns and your stores. Blessed will you be in your coming in, and blessed will you be in your going out.

The Lord will deliver your enemies who resist you, completely broken in front of you. They will come out against you one way, and they will flee from before you seven ways. The Lord will send on you his blessing in your barns, and on all on which you will put your hand, in the land which the lord of the gods gives you. The Lord raises you up for himself as a holy people, as he swore to your fathers, if you will hear the voice of the lord of the gods, and follow all his ways. All the nations of the earth will see that the name of the Lord is called on by you, and they will stand in awe of you.

The lord of the gods will multiply you for good, and in the offspring of your belly, and in the offspring of your livestock, and in the fruits of your land, on your land which the Lord swore to your fathers to give to you. May the Lord open to you his good treasury in the sky, to give rain to your land in season, may he bless all the works of your hands, so you will lend to many nations, but you will not borrow, and you will rule over many nations, but they will not rule over you.

The lord of the gods will make you the head, and not the tail, and you will then be above and you will not be below, if you will listen to the voice of the lord of the gods, in all things that I order you this day to observe. You will not turn aside from any of the commandments, which I order you today, to the right hand or to the left, to follow other gods to serve them.

But it will happen, if you will not listen to the voice of the lord of the gods, to observe all his commandments, as many as I order you today, then all these curses will come on you, and destroy you. You will be cursed in the city and You will be cursed in the field. Your barns and your stores will be cursed. Your offspring will be cursed, and the fruits of your land, your herds of oxen, and your flocks of sheep. You will be cursed in your coming in and you will be cursed in your going out.

The Lord sends against you poverty, and famine, and wasting of all things on which you will put your hand until he has completely destroyed you, and until he has consumed you quickly because of your evil devices, because you have forsaken me.

The Lord causes pestilence to cling to you until he has consumed you off the land into which you go to inherit.

# CHAPTER 28

The Lord plague you with distress, and fever, cold, inflammation, blighting, and paleness, and they will pursue you until they have destroyed you.

You have over your head a sky of brass, and the earth under you will be iron. The lord of the gods will make the rain in your land dust, and dust will come down from the sky until it has destroyed you, and until it has quickly consumed you.

The Lord gives you up for slaughter before your enemies. You go out against them one way and flee from before them seven ways, and you will be a diaspora in all the kingdoms of the earth. Your dead men will be food for the birds of the sky, and to the beasts of the earth, and there will be none to scare them away.

The Lord plague you with the ulcer of Egypt, and hemorrhoids, and with malignant scabs, and itch, so that you can not be healed.

The Lord plague you with insanity, and blindness, and astonishment of mind. You will grope at midday, as a blind man would grope in the darkness, and you will not prosper in your ways, and then you will be unjustly treated and plundered continually, and there will be no helper.

You will take a wife, and another man will have her.

You will build a house, and you will not live in it.

You will plant a vineyard, and will not gather the grapes of it.

# CHAPTER 28

Your calf will be slain before you, and you will not eat of it.

Your donkey will be violently taken away from you, and will not be restored to you.

Your sheep will be given to your enemies.

You will have no helper.

Your sons and your daughters will be given to another nation.

Your failing eyes will look for them.

Your hand has no strength.

A nation which you don't know will eat the produce of your land, and all your labors.

You will be injured and crushed always.

You will be distracted, because of the sights of your eyes which you will see.

The Lord kills you with an evil sore, on the knees and the legs, so that you will not be able to be healed from the sole of your foot to the crown of your head.

The Lord carry away you and your kings, who you will elect above you, to a nation which neither you nor your fathers know, and there you will serve other gods of wood and stone. And you will be there for a wonder, and a parable, and a tale, among all the nations, to which the lord of the gods will carry you away.

# CHAPTER 28

You will carry out much seed into the field, and you will bring in little because the locust will devour it.

You will plant a vineyard, and dress it, and will not drink the wine, neither will you delight yourself with it, because the worm will devour them.

You have olive trees in all your borders, and you will not anoint yourself with oil, because your olive will completely drop its fruit.

You will father sons and daughters, and they will not be yours, for they will be sold into captivity.

All your trees and the fruits of your land will be consumed in blight.

The stranger that is among you will be raised up very high, and you will come down very low. He will lend to you, and you will not lend to him. He will be the head, and you will be the tail.

All these curses will come on you, and will pursue you, and will destroy you until he has consumed you, and until he has destroyed you, because you did not listen to the voice of the lord of the gods, to keep his commands and his ordinances which he has commanded you.

These things will be signs for you, and wonders among your descendants forever, because you did not serve the lord of the gods with gladness and a good heart, because of the abundance of all things. You will serve your enemies, which the Lord will send out against you, in hunger, and in thirst, and in nakedness, and in the want of all things, and you will wear on your neck a yoke of iron until he has destroyed you.

The Lord will bring on you a nation from the extremity of the earth, like the swift flying of an eagle, a nation whose voice you will not understand, a nation bold in countenance, which will not wonder at the body of the aged and will not pity the young.

He will eat up the young of your livestock, and the fruits of your land, so as not to leave to you grain, wine, oil, your ox herds, and your sheep flocks, until he has destroyed you, and has completely crushed you in your cities, until the high and strong walls in which you trust are destroyed, throughout all your land, and he will plague you in your cities, which he has given to you.

You will eat the fruit of your belly, the flesh of your sons and of your daughters, all that he has given you, in your straightness and your affliction, with which your enemy will torment you.

He that is tender and very delicate among you will look with an evil eye on his brother, and the wife in his chest, and the children that are left, which may have been left to him, so as not to give to one of them of the flesh of his children, whom he will eat, because of his having nothing left him in your straightness, and in your affliction, with which your enemies will afflict you in all your cities.

She that is tender and delicate among you, whose foot has not assayed to go on the earth for delicacy and tenderness, will look with an evil eye on her husband in her chest, and her son and her daughter, and her afterbirth that comes out between her feet, and the child which she will carry, for she will eat them because of the want of all things, secretly in your straightness, and in your affliction, with which your enemy will afflict you in your cities.

If you will not listen to all the words of this law, which have been written in this book, to fear this glorious and wonderful name, (this is Yahweh your god),[1] then the Lord will magnify your plagues, and the plagues of your seed, great and wonderful plagues, and evil and abiding diseases.

He will bring on you all the evil pain of Egypt, of which you were afraid, and they will cling to you. The Lord will bring on you every sickness, and every plague that is not written, and everyone that is written in the book of this law until he has destroyed you.

You will be left few in number, whereas you were as the stars of the sky in number because you did not listen to the voice of the lord of the gods. It will come to pass that as the Lord rejoiced to do you good and to multiply you, so the Lord will rejoice to destroy you, and you will be quickly removed from the land into which you go to inherit.

The lord of the gods will scatter you among all nations, from one end of the earth to the other, and there you will serve other gods of wood and stone, which you have not known, nor your fathers. Moreover, among those nations he will not give you quiet, nor will the sole of your foot have

# CHAPTER 28

rest, and there the Lord will give you another and a misgiving heart, and failing eyes, and a wasting mind.

Your life will be in suspense before your eyes, and you will be afraid by day and by night, and you will have no assurance of your life. In the morning you will say, "If only it were evening!" and in the evening you will say, "If only it were morning!" for the fear of your heart with which you will fear, and for the sights of your eyes which you will see.

The Lord will bring you back to Egypt in ships, by the way of which I said, "You will not see it again, and you will be sold there to your enemies as slave-men and slave-women, but none will buy you."

## CHAPTER 28 NOTES

**1** LXX 963: touto kurion ton ṯeon sou (ΤΟΥΤΟ ΚΥΡΙΟΝ ΤΟΝ ΘΕΟΝϹΟΥ). Translation: himself lord the god yours

• LXX 53: touto KU tou ṮU sou (ⲧⲟⲧⲟ ΚΥ ⲧⲱ ΘΥ ⲥⲟⲩ). Translation: himself lord the god yours

• LXX 392: autou kúrion tòn ṯeón sou (Αυⲧⲟ ⳑⲩβιⲱ ⲧⲱ Θ6ⲱ ⲥⲟⲩ). Translation: this lord the god yours

• Leningrad Codex: hazzeh 'ēt Yəhwâ 'ĕlōhêkā (הַזֶּה אֶת יְהוָה אֱלֹהֶיךָ). Translation: this is (in Aramaic, or you in Punic) Yahweh your god

• Shapiro Scroll: phrase missing

• Peshitta: dmryå ålwkn (ܕܡܪܝܐ ܐܠܘܟܢ). Translation: the master god yours

- Targum Onkelos: yāt Yyā 'ĕlāhāk (יָת יְיָ אֱלָהָךְ). Translation: it's Yahweh your god
- Targum Pseudo-Jonathan: yat Yyā 'ĕlāhākôn (יָת יְיָ אֱלָהְכוֹן). Translation: it's Yahweh your gods
- Sahidic manuscript 17: fai pe joeis peknoute (ϥⲁⲓ ⲡⲉ ϫⲟⲉⲓⲥ ⲡⲉⲕⲛⲟⲩⲧⲉ). Translation: it's sky (or heaven) master your (or our, his, her) god
- Bohairic manuscripts: fai pe phois peknout (Ϥⲁⲓ ⲡⲉ ⲡϬⲟⲓⲥ ⲡⲉⲕⲛⲟⲩϯ). Translation: it's is lord your (or our, his, her) god

The phrase was injected at some point into the text; however, it is likely that there was originally a name here. The only indicator of what that might have been is in the Sahidic manuscripts, which suggest the name may have been Shamayim. The phrase is not found in the Shapira Scroll, which does use the name Yahweh; however, the Shapira Scroll's chapter 28 is quite structurally different than the Leningrad Codex, and there is no clear parallel verse. As the verse is in all other sources, and the only name present in the texts is Yahweh, that name is used here.

# CHAPTER 29

These are the words of the covenant, which the Lord commanded Moses to make with the children of Israel in the land of Moab, besides the covenant which he made with them in Horeb. Moses called all the sons of Israel and said to them, "You have seen all things that the Lord did in the land of Egypt before you to Pharaoh and his servants, and all his land, the great temptations which your eyes have seen, the signs, and those great wonders. Yet the lord of the gods has not given you the heart to know, and eyes to see, and ears to hear, until this day. He led you forty years in the wilderness, your garments did not grow old, and your sandals were not worn away off your feet. You did not eat bread, you did not drink wine or strong drink, that you might know that I am the lord of the gods. You came as far as this place, and there came out Sihon king of Heshbon, and Og king of Bashan, to meet us in war. We destroyed them and took their land, and I gave it as an inheritance to Reuben and Gad, and the half-tribe of Manasseh.

You will make sure to do all the words of this covenant, that you may understand all things that you will do. You all stand today before the lord of the gods, the heads of your tribes, and your elders, and your judges, and your officers, every man of Israel, your wives, and your children, and the stranger who is among your camp, from your lumberjack to your water collector, that you should enter into the covenant of the lord of the gods and his oaths, as many as the lord of the gods appoints you today. He will appoint you for himself as a people, and he will be your god, as he said to you, and as he swore to your fathers, Abraham, and Isaac, and Jacob.

I do not appoint to you alone this covenant and this oath, but to those also who are here with you today before the lord of the gods, and to those who are not here with you today. For you know how we lived in the land of Egypt, and how we came through the middle of the nations through whom you came. You saw their abominations, and their idols, wood and stone, silver and gold, which are among them. In case there be among you man, or woman, or family, or tribe, whose heart has turned aside from the lord of the gods, having gone to serve the gods of these nations. If there is among you a root springing up with gall and bitterness.

It will be if one will hear the words of this curse, and will flatter himself in his heart, saying, "Let good happen to me, for I will walk in the error of my heart," in case the sinner destroy the guiltless with him, god will by no means be willing to pardon him, but then the anger of the Lord and his jealousy will flame out against that man, and all the curses of this covenant will attach themselves to him, which are written in this book, and the Lord will blot out his name from under the sky. The Lord will separate that man for the evil of all the children of Israel, according to all the curses of the covenant that are written in the book of this law.

Another generation will say, even your sons who will rise after you, and the stranger who will come from a land far away, and will see the plagues of that land and their diseases, which the Lord has sent on it, brimstone and burning salt, (the whole land will not be sown, neither will any green thing spring, nor rise on it, as Sodom and Gomorrah were destroyed, and Admah and Zeboiim which the Lord overthrew in his rage and anger) and all the nations will say, "Why has the Lord done this to this land? What is this great fierceness of anger?"

Men will say, "Because they abandoned the covenant of the lord of the gods of their fathers, the things which he appointed to their fathers when he brought them out of the land of Egypt, and they went and served other gods, which they did not know, and he did not assign them to them. The Lord was exceedingly angry with that land to bring on it according to all the curses which are written in the book of this law. The Lord removed them from their land in rage and anger, and very great indignation, and threw them out into another land," as at present. The secret things belong to our the lord of the gods, but the things that are revealed belong to us and to our children forever to follow all the words of this law.

# CHAPTER 30

It will come to pass when all these things have happened to you, the blessing and the curse, which I have set in front of you, and you will receive them into your heart among all the nations, in which the Lord has scattered you, and will return to the lord of the gods, and will listen to his voice, according to all things which I order you this day, with all your heart, and with all your mind, then the Lord will heal your iniquities, and will pity you, and will again gather you out from all the nations, among which the Lord has scattered you. If your dispersion is from one end of the sky to the other, there the lord of the gods will gather you, and there will the lord of the gods take you. The lord of the gods will bring you in from there into the land which your fathers have inherited, and you will inherit it, and he will treat you well, and multiply you more than your fathers.

The Lord will purge your heart, and the heart of your seed, to love the lord of the gods with all your heart, and with all your mind, that you may live. The lord of the gods will put these curses on your enemies, and on those that hate you, who have persecuted you. You will return and listen to the voice of the lord of the gods and will keep his commands, all that I order you this day. The lord of the gods will bless you in every work of your hands, in the offspring of your belly, and the offspring of your livestock, and in the fruits of your land, because the lord of the gods will again rejoice over you for good, as he rejoiced over your fathers. If you will listen to the voice of the lord of the gods, to keep his commandments, and his ordinances, and his judgments written in the book of this law, if you turn to the lord of the gods with all your heart, and with all your mind.

This command which I give you this day is not difficult, neither is it far from you. It is not in the sky above, as if someone was asking, "Who will go up for us into the sky, and will take it for us, and we will hear and do it?" Neither is it beyond the sea, saying, "Who will go over for us to the other side of the sea, and take it for us, and make it known to us, and we will do it?" The word is very near you, in your mouth, and your heart, and in your hands to do it. Look, I have set before you this day life and death, good and evil. If you will listen to the commands of the lord of the gods, which I command you this day, to love the lord of the gods, to follow all his ways, and to keep his ordinances, and his judgments, and then you will live and will be many in number, and the lord of the gods will bless you in all the land into which you go to inherit it.

But if your heart changes, and you will not listen, and you will go astray and worship other gods, and serve them, I declare to you this day, that you will completely perish, and you will by no means live long on the land, into which you cross over the Jordan to inherit. I call both the sky and earth to witness this day against you, I have set before you life and death, the blessing and the curse. Choose your life, that you and your seed may live, to love the lord of the gods, to listen to his voice, and cling to him, for this is your life, and the length of your days, that you should live on the land, which the Lord swore to your fathers, Abraham, and Isaac, and Jacob, to give to them.

# CHAPTER 31

Moses finished speaking all these words to all the children of Israel, and said to them, "I am today a hundred and twenty years old. I will not be able any longer to come in or go out. The Lord said to me, 'You will not go over this Jordan.' The lord of the gods who goes before you will destroy these nations before you, and you will inherit them. It will be Joshua that leads you, as the Lord has said. The lord of the gods will do to them as he did to Sihon and Og the two kings of the Amorites, who were beyond Jordan, and to their land, as he destroyed them. The Lord has delivered them to you, and you will do to them, as I ordered you. Be courageous and strong. Don't be afraid or cowardly before them, as it is the lord of the gods that advances with you, among you, and he will not abandon you or desert you."

Moses called Joshua, and said to him before all Israel, "Be courageous and strong, for you will go in before these people into the land which the Lord swore to give to your fathers, and you will give it to them for an inheritance. The Lord that goes with you will not betray you or abandon you, and don't be afraid," therefore don't be afraid.

Moses wrote the words of this law in a book and gave it to the priests the sons of Levi who carry the box of the covenant of the Lord, and to the elders of the sons of Israel. Moses ordered them in that day, "After seven years, in the time of the year of release, in the feast of tabernacles, when all Israel comes together to appear before the lord of the gods, in the place which the Lord will choose, you will read this law before all Israel, having assembled the people, the men, and the women, the children, and the stranger that is in your cities, that they may hear, and that they may learn to fear the lord of the gods. They will listen to all the words of this law. Their sons who have not known will hear, and will learn to fear the lord of the gods all the days that they live on the land, into which you go over Jordan to inherit."

The Lord said to Moses, "Look, the days of your death are at hand, call Joshua, and stand by the doors of the tabernacle of testimony, and I will give him an order."

Moses and Joshua went to the tabernacle of testimony and stood by the doors of the tabernacle of testimony. The Lord descended in a cloud and stood by the doors of the tabernacle of testimony, and the pillar of the cloud stood by the doors of the tabernacle of testimony. The Lord said to Moses, "Look, you will sleep with your fathers, and these people will rise and go whoring after the alien gods of the land, into which they are entering, and they will forsake me, and break my covenant, which I made with them. I will be very angry with them on that day, and I will leave them and turn my face away from them, and they will be devoured. Many evils and plagues will come on them, and they will say in that day, 'Because my lord of the gods is not with me, these evils have come on me.' I will certainly turn away my face from them in that day, because of all their evil doings which they have done, because they turned aside after alien gods. Now write the words of this song, and teach it to the children of Israel, and you will put it into their mouth, that this song may witness for me among the children of Israel to their face. For I will bring them into the good land, which I swore to their fathers, to give to them a land flowing with milk and honey, and they will eat and be filled and satisfy themselves. Then they will turn aside after other gods, and serve them, and they will provoke me, and break my covenant. This song will stand up to witness against them, for they will not forget it out of their mouth, or out of the mouth of their seed. I know their wickedness, what they are doing here today before I have brought them into the good land, which I swore to their fathers."

Moses wrote this song on that day and taught it to the children of Israel. He ordered Joshua, "Be courageous and strong, for you will bring the sons of Israel into the land, which the Lord swore to them, and he will be with you."

When Moses finished writing all the words of this law in a book, even to the end, then he ordered the Levites who bear the box of the covenant of the Lord, "Take the book of this law, and you will put it inside of the box of the covenant of the lord of the gods, and it will be there among you as a testimony. For I know your provocation, and your stiff neck, for yet during my life with you at this day, you have been provoking in your conduct toward god, so how will you not also be so after my death? Gather together to me the heads of your tribes, and your elders, and your judges, and your officers, that I may speak in their ears all these words, and I call both the sky and earth to witness against them. For I know that after my death you will completely transgress, and turn aside out of the way which I have commanded you, and evils will come on you at the end of days because you will do evil before the Lord, to provoke him to anger by the works of your hands."

Moses spoke all the words of this song even to the end, in the ears of the whole assembly.

# CHAPTER 32

Watch Shamayim,[1] and I will speak, and let Eretz[2] hear the words out of my mouth. Let my speech be looked for like the rain, and my words come down as dew, as the shower on the plants, and as snow on the grass. For I have called on the name of the Lord, "Assign you greatness to our God. As for God, his works are true, and all his ways are judgments, God is faithful, and there is no unrighteousness in him. Just and holy is the Lord. They have sinned, not pleasing him, spotted children, a contrary and perverse generation. Do you, therefore, repay the Lord? Are the people so foolish and unwise? Did not your father purchase you, and make you, and form you?"

Remember the days of old, consider the ages of ages. Ask your father, and he will tell you, your elders, and they will tell you. When the Highest[3] divided the nations, when he separated the sons of Adam, he divided the borders of the nations according to the number of the messengers of God. The people of Jacob became the portion of the Lord, and Israel was the line of his inheritance. He maintained him in the wilderness, in burning thirst and dry land. He led him about and instructed him, and kept him as the apple of his eye. As an eagle would watch over his brood and yearns over his young, and receives them having spread his wings, and takes them up on his back. The Lord alone led them, there was no alien god with them.

He brought them up on the strength of the land. He fed them with the fruits of the fields. They sucked honey out of the rock, and oil out of the solid rock. Butter of cows, and milk of sheep, with the fat of lambs and rams, of calves and kids, with the fat of kidneys of wheat, and he drank wine, the blood of the grape. So Jacob ate and was filled, and the beloved one kicked, he grew fat, he became thick and broad. Then he abandoned the god that made him and departed from God his savior. They provoked me to anger with alien gods, with their abominations, they bitterly angered me. They sacrificed to devils, and not to God, but to gods whom they did not know. New and fresh gods came in, who their fathers did not know.

You have forsaken the God who fathered you and forgotten El[4] who feeds you. The Lord saw, and was jealous, and was provoked by the anger of his sons and daughters, and said, "I will turn away my face from them, and will show what will happen to them in the last days, for it is a perverse generation, sons with no faith. They have provoked me to jealousy with that which is not God, they have exasperated me with their idols, and I will provoke them to jealousy with them that are no nation, I will anger them with a nation void of understanding. For a fire has been started out of my anger, it will burn to Hades below, it will devour the land and the fruits of it. It will set on fire the foundations of the mountains. I will gather evils on them and will paralyze them with my weapons. They will be wasted by hunger and devoured by Resheph,[5] and destroyed bitterly. I will send out against them the teeth of a hippopotamus,[6] with the rage of serpents creeping on the ground. Outside, the sword will bereave them of children, and terror will issue out of the secret chambers. The young man will perish with the virgin, the suckling with he who has grown old."

I said, "I will scatter them, and I will cause their memorial to cease from among men. Were it not for the anger of the enemy, in case they should live long, in case their enemies should combine against them, in case they should say, 'Our own high arm, and not the Lord, has done all these things.'"

It is a nation that has lost counsel, and there is no understanding in them. They had no sense to understand. Let them reserve these things against the time to come. How should one pursue a thousand, and two chase tens of thousands, if God had not sold them, and the Lord delivered them up? For their gods are not like our god, but our enemies are void of understanding. For their vine is of the vine of Sodom, and their vine-branch of Gomorrah, their grape is a grape of gall, their cluster is one of bitterness. Their wine is the rage of serpents and the incurable rage of asps.

Look! Are not these things stored up by me, and sealed among my treasures? In the day of vengeance, I will repay, whenever their foot will be tripped up. The day of their destruction is near to them, and the judgments at hand are close to you. The Lord will judge his people and will be comforted over his servants. For he saw that they were paralyzed, and failed in the hostile invasion, and were become feeble.

The Lord asked, "Where are their gods in whom they trusted? The fat of whose sacrifices you ate, and you drank the wine of their drink offerings? Let them rise and help you, and be your protectors. Look, Look that I am he, and there is no god beside me. I kill, and I will make live. I will kill, and I will heal. None will deliver out of my hands. For I will lift my hand to the sky, and swear by my right hand, and I will say, I live forever. I will sharpen my sword like lightning, and my hand will take hold of judgment. I will render judgment to my enemies and will repay them that hate me. I will make my weapons drunk with blood, and my sword will devour flesh, it will glut itself with the blood of the wounded, and from the captivity of the heads of their enemies that rule over them."

Celebrate Shamayim with him, and worship him all the sons of God. Celebrate nations, with all your people, and strengthen him all messengers of God.[7] He will avenge the blood of his sons, and he will render vengeance, and repay justice to his enemies, and will reward them that hate him, and the Lord will purge the land of his people.

Moses wrote this song on that day and taught it to the children of Israel, and Moses went in and spoke all the words of this law in the ears of the people, he and Joshua the son of Nun. Moses finished speaking to all Israel. He said to them, "Pay attention with your heart to all these words, which I testify to you this day, which you will command your sons, to observe and do all the words of this law. For this is no vain word to you, for it is your life, and because of this word you will live long on the land, into which you go over Jordan to inherit."

The Lord said to Moses in this day, "Go up to Mount Abarim, (this is Mount Nebo which is in the land of Moab near Jericho), and see the land of Canaan, which I give to the sons of Israel, and die in the mountain where you are going, and be added to your people, as Aaron your brother died on Mount Horeb and was added to his people. Because you disobeyed my word among the children of Israel, at the waters of Temptation of Kadesh in the wilderness of Sin, because you did not praise me among the sons of Israel. You will see the land before you, but you will not enter into it."

## CHAPTER 32 NOTES

**1** Codex Vaticanus: ourane (ΟΥΡΑΝΕ). Translation: sky (or Uranus)

• Aleppo Codex: Šmym (שמים). Translation: Shamayim (or skies)

• Leningrad Codex: šāmayim (שָׁמַיִם). Translation: Shamayim (or skies)

• Peshitta: šmyå (ܫܡܝܐ). Translation: sky

• Targum Onkelos: šəmayyā' (שְׁמַיָּא). Translation: sky

• Targum Jerusalem: šāmayim (שָׁמַיִם). Translation: skies

• Targum Pseudo-Jonathan: šəmayā' (שְׁמַיָּא). Translation: sky

• Sahidic manuscript 17: pe (ⲡⲉ). Translation: sky

Shamayim was depicted as the same type of primordial deity in the Septuagint as Uranus was in the Greek myths and called on to witness blessings and curses, implying consciousness. Based on the writings of Jonah and Zephaniah, as well as *4ᵗʰ Kingdoms* (Masoretic Kings), Shamayim was a major god in Samaria and Judea before King Josiah's reforms and therefore his name is restored from the Masoretic texts, as he was not known as Uranus.

**2** Codex Vaticanus: Gē (ΓΗ). Translation: Ge (or land, dirt, earth)

• Aleppo Codex: Års (אֶרֶץ). Translation: Eretz (or land, earth, dirt)

• Leningrad Codex: 'Āreṣ (אֶרֶץ). Translation: Eretz (or land, earth, dirt)

• Peshitta: årôå (ܐܪܥܐ). Translation: land

• Targum Onkelos: 'ar'ā' (אַרְעָא). Translation: land

• Targum Jerusalem: 'ar'ā' (אַרְעָא). Translation: land

• Targum Pseudo-Jonathan: 'ar'ā' (אַרְעָא). Translation: land

• Sahidic manuscript 17: kah (ⲕⲁϩ). Translation: land (or district)

The Earth (Eretz / Ge) is depicted as the same type of primordial deity in the Septuagint as it was in the Greek myths and called on to witness blessings and curses, implying consciousness. As her name was not Earth or Ge, the Hebrew (and Canaanite) name Eretz is restored from the Masoretic Text. The fact that she is called on by Moses, along with Shamayim, means the Song of Moses is much older than the rest of *Deuteronomy*, and must, if nothing else, date to before King Josiah banned the worship of Shamayim, in circa 628 BCE.

**3** Codex Vaticanus: upsitos (ΥΨΙⲤⲦⲞⲤ). Translation: highest

• Aleppo Codex: ôlywn (עֶלְיוֹן). Translation: highest

• Leningrad Codex: 'elyôn (עֶלְיוֹן). Translation: highest

• Peshitta: mrymå (ܡܪܝܡܐ). Translation: command

• Targum Onkelos: 'illā'â (עִלָּאָה). Translation: highest

# CHAPTER 32

- Targum Jerusalem: 'îlayā' (עִילָיָא)

- Targum Pseudo-Jonathan: 'ilā'â 'almā' (עָלְאָה עָלְמָא). Translation: highest eternal

- Sahidic manuscript 17: pnoute (ⲡⲛⲟⲩⲧⲉ). Translation: the god

El Elyon (Highest God) was God of Melchizedek, the king of Salem (either Jerusalem or the city of Salem in Samaria) when Abraham passed through Canaan. The term El Elyon is known to have been a major god of the Canaanites, called Ål wÓlyn in the Sefire Treaty from circa 750 BCE. The quotes of Sanchuniathon's writing that have survived to the present, from circa 1200 BCE, referred to the god called Elioun as the primordial creator-god of the Canaanites.

**4** Codex Vaticanus: ṬU (ⲐⲨ). Translation: God

- Septuagint manuscript 246: ṭu sou (θυ σου). Translation: god yours

- Aleppo Codex: Ål (אֵל). Translation: El (or God)

- Leningrad Codex: El (אֵל). Translation: El (or God)

- Peshitta: ålhå (ܐܠܗܐ). Translation: god

- Targum Onkelos: 'ĕlāhā' (אֱלָהָא). Translation: highest

- Targum Jerusalem: Yəyā (??). Translation: Yahweh

- Targum Pseudo-Jonathan: Yəyā (??). Translation: Yahweh

- Sahidic manuscript 17: pnoute (ⲡⲛⲟⲩⲧⲉ). Translation: the god

This verse shows the Greeks did translate the term El as God (θεου). As El is a proper name, it is restored from the Masoretic texts in this translation.

**5** Codex Vaticanus: orneōn (ⲞⲢⲚⲈⲰⲚ). Translation: raptor (or bird of prey)

- Aleppo Codex: Ršp (רשף). Translation: Resheph (or pestilence)

- Leningrad Codex: Rešep (רֶשֶׁף). Translation: Resheph

- Peshitta: rwḥå byštå (ܪܘܚܐ ܒܝܫܬܐ). Translation: wind (or spirit) of evil

- Targum Onkelos: rûḥîn bîšān (רוּחִין בִּישָׁן). Translation: winds (or spirits) of evil

- Targum Jerusalem: ḥarbā' (חַרְבָּא). Translation: sword (or dagger)

- Targum Pseudo-Jonathan: lîlîn ûmərawwḥê rəwāwḥin bîšîn (לִילִין וּמְרָוְוחֵי רְוָוחִין בִּישִׁין). Translation: night-demons and rebellious winds (or spirits) of evil

- Sahidic manuscript 17: halate (ϩⲁⲗⲁⲧⲉ). Translation: flying creatures (or birds)

Resheph was the Amorite god of both pestilence and healing, whose name was recorded as Rašaap (𒊑𒀸𒀊) in tablets from Ebla dating to the 3rd millennium BCE, as well as Ršpw (𓂋𓈙𓊪𓅱) in Egyptian. Resheph's name was later recorded as Ršp (𒊑𒅖𒉺) in Ugaritic Canaanite from the 1300s BCE, and Ršp (𐤓𐤔𐤐) in Phoenician Canaanite from the early iron age, both of which are direct transliterations of the Classical Hebrew Ršp (רשף). Resheph was recorded as the husband of Adamma, the Amorite, and later Hurrian and Edomite goddess of the earth, the name used in *Numbers* for the Israelite earth goddess.

Resheph was one of the major gods of the Hyksos dynasty, considered the equivalent of the Babylonian god Nergal (𒀭𒄿𒄄𒄊) and Egyptian Sutekh (𓋴𓏏𓈙), originally pronounced as stš before the New Kingdom era, and later as stǩ, which resulted in the later Greek transliteration of Sēth (Σηθ). After the collapse of the Hyksos dynasty, the worship of both Sutekh and Resheph was suppress during the early New Kingdom era, and a new god named Shed (�) largely replaced Resheph in Canaan, which appears to be the origin of the Canaanite term šd (𐤔𐤃) and the Israelite name Šdy (𐤔𐤃𐤉). The inclusion of the name in the Song of

# CHAPTER 32

Moses indicates that the song was likely composed before the suppression of Resheph during the New Kingdom era.

**6** Codex Vaticanus: t̠ēriōn (ⲐⲎⲢⲒⲰⲚ). Translation: wild animals (or Lupus)

- Aleppo Codex: bhmt (**כהמת**). Translation: animal (or livestock)

- Leningrad Codex: bəhēmôt (בְּהֵמוֹת). Translation: behemoth

- Peshitta: ḥywty šnå (ܚܝܘ̈ܬܐ ,ܫܢܐ). Translation: animals (or living) tusks (or teeth)

- Targum Onkelos: ḥêwat bārā' (חֵיוַת בָּרָא). Translation: animal of forest (or prairie)

- Targum Jerusalem: ḥêwat bərā' (חֵיוַת בְּרָא). Translation: animal of forest (or prairie)

- Targum Pseudo-Jonathan: 'Akkûyym dinkîtîn bəšînêhôn hêk hêwawt bərā' (עַכּוֹיִים דְּנָכִיתִין בְּשִׁינֵיהוֹן הֵיךְ חֵיוֹת בְּרָא). Translation: Acreans who bite with teeth like animals of the forest

- Sahidic manuscript 17: t̠ērion (ⲐⲎⲢⲒⲞⲚ). Translation: feral animals

The translation of "wild animals" (θηρίων) found in the Septuagint, mirrors the terms found in the Aleppo and Leningrad codices, Peshitta, and most targums. The Targum Pseudo-Jonathan switched this to the people from Acre, a city on the coast of modern Israel. Ȯkw (𓊪𓈎𓅱) was an ancient Phoenician city, already having the name of Ȯkå (𓊪𓈎𓅱) during the Egyptian Old Kingdom era. The city was called Ȯkw until the Greeks took control of the region. Before they took control of the region, the city had been known as Akē (Ακη) in Greek, and associated with the myth of Heracles. After taking control of the region, the Greeks renamed it Antioķeia Ptolemais (Αντιοχεια Πτολεμαις), although this was shortened to Ptolemais (Πτολεμαις) in 260 BCE. This name was adopted into Hebrew and Judeo-Aramaic as Ptwlmåws (פטולמאוס),

which suggests the edit dates to earlier than the Greek conquest of the Persian Empire. During the Persian era, there was a major Persian fortress at Ókw, which was destroyed when the Greeks conquered the region.

The word in the Aleppo Codex is identical to the word bhmt (𒁉𒂖𒋫𒁄) from the Bronze Age Ugaritic texts, which is accepted as meaning the same thing. The Leningrad Codex use a later development of the word, as behemoth (בְּהֵמוֹת). This has generally been interpreted as "livestock" by Jews, however, Christians have interpreted it several ways. In Masoretic Job, Behemoth (בְּהֵמוֹת) was the name of a monster, however, in this verse it is translated a "livestock" in almost all alternate sources.

The word was transliterated into the Peshitta's *Job* as bhmwt (ܒܗܡܘܬܐ), indicating that the earlier Imperial Aramaic spelling was almost certainly bhmwt (בהמ׳ות), the plural form of bhmw (בהמ׳ו), however, that word is not found in any known Aramaic text. For almost 2000 years, linguists have considered this a transliteration of the Ancient Egyptian word for påîhmw (𓄿𓏏𓎛𓐝𓈖), meaning "the ox of water," or "hippopotamus." This translation was worked out during the Early Christian Era, and assumed to be a reference to a hippopotamus, based on the conceptually similar words meaning hippopotamus in Greek, Arabic, Persian, Hebrew, and Coptic, all of which are composed of words meaning "horse" and either "water" or "river."

This connection was worked out in the late Classical Era, and therefore influenced the languages within the Byzantine and Russian Empires, resulting in the words for "hippopotamus" being derived from behemoth in many languages, including Armenian begemot (բեգեմոտ), Azerbaijani begemot, Belarusian behemót (бегемо́т), Bulgarian begemót (бегемо́т), Chuvash begemot (бегемот), Georgian behemoti (ბეჰემოთი), Hebrew behemót

(בְּהֵמוֹת), Kazakh begemot (бегемот), Kyrgyz begemot (бегемот), Latvian behemots, Lithuanian begemotas, Ossetian begemot (бегемот), Russian begemót (бегемо́т), Tajik bahmut (бахмут), Turkmen begemot, Ukrainian behemót (бегемо́т), Uyghur bëgëmot (بېگېموت), and Uzbek begemot. In some of these languages, the term is now considered dated and has been replaced with words based on the Greek word hippopotamos (ἱπποπόταμος).

The Ancient Egyptians had several names for "hippopotamus," however, generally called it a kảb (𓂝𓃀𓄿𓄭), and therefore, it suggests that the Song of Moses was composed in an Egyptianized Canaanite dialect earlier than the New Kingdom era, when the term ss-yảwr (𓇌𓃀𓈀 𓏤𓏤), meaning 'horse of the Nile,' was adopted by the Canaanites as a name for the hippopotamus.

The earliest documented Canaanite word for horse, was the late Bronze Age sśw (𒐊𒈽𒄘) in Ugaritic, which was imported to Egyptian as ssm ( 𓏴 𓋴𓅓), meaning "horse." Conversely, yảwr (𓇌𓈀) was imported to Canaanite from the Egyptian ỉtrw (𓇋𓏏𓂋𓈗), meaning "great river," and specifically referring to the Nile.

The Egyptian term continued in use until the Classical era, when it was spelled as hto-ior (ϩⲧⲟ ⲓⲟⲣ), meaning "horse" and "Nile" in Coptic Egyptian. The Canaanite term was also imported to Median and Persian as "aspa ap" from the Avestan words aspa (سپرنسب) and ap (سپ), meaning "horse" and "water," and continues today in the Persian term for hippopotamus, asb-e âbi (اسب آبی). The Persian term appears to have been the basis of the Greek and Arabic terms hippopotamos (ἱπποπόταμος) and faras nahr (فرس نهر), both of which combine the words for "horse" and "river."

In this verse, the Greek translation could also be interpreted as a reference to the constellation Lupus, however, it is unlikely that the original Canaanite song of Moses was referring to an asterism, and so the translation of "hippopotamus" is imported from the

# CHAPTER 32

Leningrad Codex via the accepted Middle Egyptian interpretation of the word.

**7** Codex Vaticanus: eufran̲t̲ēte ouranoi ama autō kai proskunēsatōsan autō pantes uioi T̄U̅ (ΕΥΦΡΑΝΘΗΤΕΟΥΡΑΝΟΙΑΜΑ ΑΥΤѠ ΚΑΙ ΠΡΟϹΚΥΝΗϹΑΤѠϹΑΝ ΑΥΤѠ ΠΑΝΤΕϹ ΥΙΟΙ Θ̅Υ̅). Translation: Praise skies (or Uranus) together with him and worship him all the sons of god

• Septuagint manuscript 58: eufran̲t̲ēte oi ouranoi ama autō kao proskunēsatōsan autō pantes uioi t̲eou (ᴆʋᵬϱₐₙθₗₜϭ Θ ουϱₐₙΘ ᴧμα ᴧυτοο ʟₐ/ πϱϭτᴜᴜᴌₐϲₐτοοϭᴆ ᴧυτοο πᴆυτϭ́ς yΘ θϭου). Translation: praise the skies (or Uranus) together with him and worship him all the sons of god

• Septuagint manuscript 407: eufran̲t̲ēte ouranoi ama autois kai proskunēsatōsan auton pantes uioi t̲eou (ᴆʋᵬϱₐₙθₗₜϭ ουϱₐₙΘ ᴧμα ᴧυτΘς ʟₐ/ πϱϭτᴜᴜᴌₐϲₐτοοϭᴆ ᴧυτΘ πᴆυτϭ́ς yΘ θϭου). Translation: praise the skies (or Uranus) together with them and worship him all the sons of god

• Septuagint manuscript 313: eufran̲t̲ēte ouranoi ama autō kai proskunēsatōsan autō pantes oi uioi t̲eou oi t̲eou (ᴆʋᵬϱₐₙθₗₜϭ ουϱₐₙΘ ᴧμα ᴧυτοο ʟₐ/ πϱϭτᴜᴜᴌₐϲₐτοοϭᴆ ᴧυτοο πᴆυτϭ́ς Θ yΘ θϭου Θ θϭου). Translation: praise the skies (or Uranus) together with them and worship him all the sons of god the god

• Sahidic manuscript 17: eufrane mn peflaos auō maroutajroou mmof nnangelos tērou mpoute (ΕΥΦΡΑΝΕ ΜΝ ΠΕϥλΑΟϹ ΑΥѠ ΜΑΡΟΥΤΑϪΡΟΟΥ ΜΜΟϥ ΝΝΑΓΓΕλΟϹ ΤΗΡΟΥ ΜΠΝΟΥΤΕ). Translation: rejoice will the people and witness the strength of them from the angels of the god

This verse is not found in the Masoretic texts, Peshitta, or Targums. The name Shamayim is used as it was the Masoretic translation of Uranus in other verses.

216

# CHAPTER 33

This is the blessing with which Moses the man of God blessed the children of Israel before his death. He said, "The Lord has come from Sinai, and has appeared from Seir to us, and has rushed out of the Mount of Paran, with the ten thousands of Kadesh, on his right hand were his messengers with him. He spared his people, and all his sanctified ones are under your hands, and they are under you, and he received from his words the law which Moses ordered us, an inheritance to the assemblies of Jacob. He will be king with the beloved one when the kings of the people are gathered together with the tribes of Israel. Let Reuben live, and not die, and let him be many in number.

This is the blessing of Judah, "Hear the Lord, the voice of Judah, and you visit his people, his hands will contend for him, and you will be a help from his enemies."

To Levi, he said, "Give to Levi his manifestations, and his truth to the holy man, whom they tempted in the temptation. They criticized him at the water of strife. Who says to his father and mother, I have not seen you, and he did not know his brothers, and he refused to know his sons. He kept your oracles and observed your covenant. They will declare your ordinances to Jacob, and your law to Israel: they will place incense in the time of your anger continually on your altar. Bless, the Lord, his strength, and accept the works of his hands, break the loins of his enemies that have risen against him, and don't let them that hate him rise."

To Benjamin, he said, "The beloved of the Lord will live in confidence, and god overshadows him always, and he rested between his shoulders."

To Joseph, he said, "His land is of the blessing of the Lord, of the seasons of sky and dew, and of the deeps of wells below, and of the fruits of the changes of the sun in season, and of the produce of the months, from the top of the ancient mountains, and from the top of the eternal hills, and of the fullness of the land in season, and let the things pleasing to him that lived in the bush come on the head of Joseph, and on the crown of him who was glorified above his brothers. His beauty is as the firstborn of his bull, his horn is the horn of a rhinoceros,[1] with them he will thrust the nations at once, even from the end of the earth, these are the ten thousands of Ephraim, and these are the thousands of Manasseh."

To Zebulun, he said, "Rejoice Zebulun, in your going out, and Issachar in his tents. They will completely destroy the nations, and you will call men there, and there offer the sacrifice of righteousness, for the wealth of the sea will suckle you, and so will the marts of them that live by the sea-coast."

To Gad he said, "Blessed be he that enlarges Gad: as a lion he rested, having broken the arm and the ruler. He saw his first fruits, that there the land of the kings gathered with the chiefs of the people divided. The Lord worked righteousness and his judgment with Israel."

# CHAPTER 33

To Dan, he said, "Dan is a lion's cub, and will leap out of Bashan."

To Naphtali, he said, "Naphtali has the fullness of good things, and let him be filled with the blessings of the Lord. He will inherit the west and the south."

To Asher, he said, "Asher is blessed with children, and he will be acceptable to his brothers. He will dip his foot in oil. His sandal will be iron and brass; as your days, so will be your strength. There is not any such as the god of the beloved, who mounts the sky assists you, and the magnificence of the framework."

The rule of God will protect you, and that under the strength of the eternal arms, and he will throw out the enemy from in front of you, saying, "Perish. Israel will live in confidence alone on the land of Jacob, with grain and wine, and the sky will be misty with dew on you. Blessed are you, O Israel, who is like to you, people saved by the Lord? Your helper will hold his shield over you, and his sword is your boast, and your enemies will speak falsely to you, and you will tread on their neck."

## CHAPTER 33 NOTES

**1** Codex Vaticanus: monokerōtos (ΜΟΝΟΚΕΡѠΤΟϹ). Translation: Asian rhinoceros (or unicorn, narwhal)

- Aleppo Codex: råm (רֵאם). Translation: oryx
- Leningrad Codex: rə'ēm (רְאֵם). Translation: oryx

# CHAPTER 33

- Peshitta: rymå (ܪܝܡܐ). Translation: buffalo (or unicorn)

- Targum Onkelos: rûmā' (רוּמָא). Translation: Rome (or haughty)

- Targum Jerusalem: rîmənā' (רִימְנָא). Translation: pomegranate

- Targum Pseudo-Jonathan: ribwāwtā' (רִבְוָותָא). Translation: great-stork (or Cygnus)

- Codex Gothicus Legionensis: rhinocerotis (ʀʜɪɴᴏᴄᴇʀᴏᴛɪs). Translation: rhinoceros

- Sahidic manuscript 2006: monokerōs (ᴍᴏɴᴏᴋᴇᴩⲱᴄ). Translation: unicorn

- Sahidic manuscript 17: monokerōtos (ᴍᴏɴᴏᴋᴇᴩⲱᴛᴏᴄ). Translation: unicorn

The word rə'ēm (רְאֵם) is descended from the Akkadian rimu (𒅎𒁍) meaning wild bull, and the Ugaritic rwm (𐎗𐎆𐎎) meaning wild buffalo. The related Arabic word rīm (ريم) means oryx, however, based on the reference in Daniel, rə'ēm was probably the old name of the constellation Taurus or Ares, which is probably what the author intended, as it is difficult to imagine an oryx being described so gloriously. The translators of the Targums had diverse opinions on what this verse was about, including Romans, pomegranates, and the constellation Cygnus.

The Greek unicorn was a semi-mythical creature reported to live in India, almost certainly the Asian rhinoceros, which, unlike the African rhinoceros, only has one horn. This is the translation used in the Latin Vulgate, however, "unicorn" or "oryx" are often used in modern English translations, as it is not clear what the rə'ēm (רְאֵם) actually was.

# Chapter 34

Moses went up from Araboth Moab to the mount of Nebo, to the top of Phasga, which is near Jericho, and the Lord showed him all the mountains of Gilead to Dan, and all the land of Naphtali, and all the land of Ephraim and Manasseh, and all the land of Judah to the farthest sea, and the wilderness, and the country round about Jericho, the city of palm-trees, to Zoar.

The Lord said to Moses, "This is the land of which I swore to Abraham, and Isaac, and Jacob, saying, 'To your seed will I give it,' and I have shown it to your eyes, but you will not go in there."

So Moses the servant of the Lord died in the land of Moab by the word of the Lord. They buried him in Gai near the Temple of Peor, and no one has seen his sepulcher to this day. Moses was a hundred and twenty years old at his death, yet his eyes were not dimmed, nor were his natural powers destroyed. The children of Israel wept for Moses in Araboth of Moab at the Jordan near Jericho for thirty days, and the days of the sad mourning for Moses were completed.

Joshua the son of Nun was filled with the spirit of knowledge, for Moses had laid his hands on him, and the children of Israel listened to him, and they did as the Lord commanded Moses. There did not rise another prophet in Israel like Moses, whom the Lord knew face to face, in all the signs and wonders, which the Lord sent him to work in Egypt against Pharaoh and his servants and all his land, and the great wonders, and the mighty hand which Moses displayed before all Israel.

# Septuagint Manuscripts

The following is a list of the Septuagint manuscripts referenced in the notes for this book.

The following is a list of the Septuagint manuscripts referenced in the notes for this book.

LXX A (Codex Alexandrinus) is dated to the 5th century. It is currently located at the British Library (Royal 1 D. VIII) in London.

LXX B (Codex Vaticanus) is dated to the 4th century. It is currently located at the Vatican Library (Gr. 1209) in Vatican City.

LXX F (Codex Ambrosiano A 147) is dated to the 5th century. It is currently located at the Ambrosian Library (A. 147 inf.) in Milan.

LXX G (Codex Colberto-Sarravianus) is dated to the 4th or 5th centuries. Sections are currently located at the University Library (Voss. Graec. in qu. 8) in Leiden, National Library of France (Coisl. Gr. 17) in Paris, and the National Library of Russia (Gr. 3) in St. Petersburg.

LXX V (Codex Venetus) is dated to the 8th century. It is currently located at the Marciana Library (Gr. 1) in Venice.

LXX W$^{I}$ (Codex Freer Greek MS. V) is dated to the 5th century. It is currently located at the Smithsonian Freer Gallery of Art (Inv. Nr. 06.292) in Washington.

LXX 14 is dated to the 11th century. It is currently located at the Vatican Library (Vat. Palat. Gr. 203) in Vatican City.

LXX 16 is dated to the 11th century. It is currently located at the Laurentian Library (v. 38) in Florence.

LXX 19 is dated to the 12th century. It is currently located at the Chigi Palace (R. VI. 38) in Rome.

LXX 29 is dated to the 14th century. It is currently located at the Marciana Library (Gr. 2) in Venice.

LXX 30 is dated to the 11th or 12th centuries. It is currently located at the Casanatense Library (1444) in Rome.

LXX 46 is dated to the 15th century. It is currently located at the National Library of France (Coisl. Gr. 4) in Paris.

LXX 52 is dated to the 14th century. It is currently located at the Laurentian Library (Acquisti 44) in Florence.

LXX 54 is dated to the 13th or 14th century. It is currently located at the National Library of France (Gr. 5) in Paris.

LXX 55 is dated to the 10th century. It is currently located at the Vatican Library (Regin. Gr. 1) in Vatican City.

LXX 58 is dated to the 11th century. It is currently located at the Vatican Library (Regin. gr. 10) in Vatican City.

LXX 59 is dated to the 15th century. It is currently located at the University Library (BE 7b. 10) in Glasgow.

LXX 64 is dated to the 10th century. It is currently located at the National Library of France (Gr. 2) in Paris.

LXX 68 is dated to the 15th century. It is currently located at the Marciana Library (Gr. 5) in Venice.

LXX 71 is dated to the 13th century. It is currently located at the National Library of France (Coisl. Gr. 1) in Paris.

LXX 72 is dated to the 13th century. It is currently located at the Bodleian Library (Canonic. Gr. 35) in Oxford.

LXX 75 is dated to 1125. It is currently located at University College (52) in Oxford.

LXX 76 is dated to the 13th century. It is currently located at National Library of France (Coisl. Gr. 4) in Paris.

LXX 82 is dated to the 12th century. It is currently located at the National Library of France (Coisl. Gr. 3) in Paris.

LXX 83 is dated to the 16th century. It is currently located at the Archivo da Torre do Tombo (540. 669. 668. 671. 670.) in Lisbon.

LXX 106 is dated to the 14th century. It is currently located at the Biblioteca Comunale Ariostea (187 I-III) in Ferrara.

LXX 107 is dated to 1334. It is currently located at the Biblioteca Comunale Ariostea (188 I) in Ferrara.

LXX 108 is dated to the 13th century. It is currently located at the Vatican Library (Gr. 330) in Vatican City.

LXX 118 is dated to the 11th or 12th century. It is currently located at the National Library of France (Gr. 6) in Paris.

LXX 120 is dated to the 12th or 13th centuries. It is currently located at the Marciana Library (Gr. 23) in Venice.

LXX 121 is dated to the 10th century. It is currently located at the Marciana Library (Gr. 3) in Venice.

LXX 125 is dated to the 14th century. It is currently located at the State Historical Museum (Gr. 30) in Moscow.

LXX 130 is dated to the 12th or 13th centuries. It is currently located at the Austrian National Library (Theol. Gr. 23) in Vienna.

LXX 134 is dated to the 11th centuries. It is currently located at the Marciana Library (Plut. 5.1) in Venice.

LXX 246 is dated to 1195. It is currently located at the Vatican Library (Gr. 1238) in Vatican City.

LXX 313 is dated to the 11th century. It is currently located at the National Library of Greece (43) in Athens.

LXX 314 is dated to the 13th century. It is currently located at the National Library of Greece (44) in Athens.

LXX 318 is dated to the 10th or 11th centuries. It is currently located at the Vatopedi (598) on Mount Athos.

LXX 319 is dated to 1021. It is currently located at the Vatopedi (600) on Mount Athos.

LXX 321 is dated to the 14th century. It is currently located at the Vatopedi (603) on Mount Athos.

LXX 343 is dated to the 11th century. It is currently located at the Great Lavra (352) on Mount Athos.

LXX 370 is dated to the 11th through 14th centuries. It is currently located at the Vatican Library (Chis. R VIII 61) in Vatican City.

LXX 376 is dated to the 15th century. It is currently located at the Royal Library (Y-II-5) in El Escorial.

LXX 392 is dated to the 10th century. It is currently located at the Abbey of Saint Mary of Grottaferrata (A. γ. I) in Grottaferrata.

LXX 407 is dated to the 9th century. It is currently located at the Patriarchal Library (Τάφου 2) in Jerusalem.

LXX 417 is dated to 1103. It is currently located at the Archiepiscopal. Library (1214) in London.

LXX 422 is dated to the 12th century. It is currently located at the British Library (Add. 35123) in London.

LXX 426 is dated to the 11th century. It is currently located at the British Library (Add. 39585) in London.

LXX 458 is dated to the 12th century. It is currently located at the University Library (62) in Messina.

LXX 509 is dated to the 9th or 10th centuries. Sections are currently located at the Bodleian Library (Auct. T. inf. 2. 1) in Oxford, University Library (Add. 1879. 7) in Cambridge, British Library (Add. 20002) in London, and the National Library of Russia (Gr. 62) in St. Petersburg.

LXX 527 is dated to the 14th century. It is currently located at the Bibliothèque de l'Arsenal (Gr. 8415) in Paris.

LXX 537 is dated to the 13th century. It is currently located at the National Library of France (Coisl. Gr. 184) in Paris.

LXX 610 is dated to the 14th century. It is currently located at the National Library of France (Suppl. gr. 609) in Paris.

LXX 616 is dated to the 11th century. It is currently located at the Pelekete monastery (217) on Patmos Island.

LXX 618 is dated to the 13th century. It is currently located at the Pelekete monastery (410) on Patmos Island.

LXX 619 is dated to the 15th century. It is currently located at the Pelekete monastery (411) on Patmos Island.

LXX 630 is dated to the 10th century. It is currently located at the National Library of Russia (Gr. 673) in St. Petersburg.

LXX 646 is dated to the 12th century. It is currently located at the Vatican Library (Barber. gr. 474) in Vatican City.

LXX 669 is dated to the 14th century. It is currently located at the Vatican Library (Vat. gr. 332) in Vatican City.

LXX 707 is dated to the 10th or 11th centuries. Sections are currently located at Saint Catherine's Monastery (Codex Gr. 1) in the Sinai, and the National Library of Russia (Gr. 260) in St. Petersburg.

227

LXX 730 is dated to the 10th century. It is currently located at the Marciana Library (Gr. 15) in Venice.

LXX 761 is dated to the 13th century. It is currently located at the Zentralbibliothek (C 11) in Zürich.

LXX 767 is dated to the 13th or 14th centuries. It is currently located at the Great Lavra (603) on Mount Athos.

LXX 799 is dated to 1280. It is currently located at the National Library of Greece (2491) in Athens.

LXX 847 (Papyrus Fouad 266) appears to be a copy of a Septuagint manuscript created sometime between the 1st century BCE and 1st century CE, and then copied sometime after the 12th century. It is currently located at the Sociandé Royale de Papyrologie (Gr. P. 458) in Cairo. It is a fragment of the Papyrus Fouad 266; all three known pieces are cataloged and on display together.

LXX 848 (Papyrus Fouad 266) appears to be a copy of a Septuagint manuscript created sometime between the 1st century BCE and 1st century CE, and then copied sometime after the 12th century. It is currently located at the Sociandé Royale de Papyrologie (Gr. P. 458) in Cairo.; all three known pieces are cataloged and on display together.

LXX 920 is dated to the late 4th century CE. It is currently located at the John Rylands Library (P. Gr. 1) on Manchester.

LXX 942 (Papyrus Fouad 266) appears to be a copy of a Septuagint manuscript created sometime between the 1st century BCE and 1st century CE, and then copied sometime after the 12th century. It is currently located at the Sociandé Royale de Papyrologie (Gr. P. 458) in Cairo. It is a fragment of the Papyrus Fouad 266; all three known pieces are cataloged and on display together.

# SEPTUAGINT MANUSCRIPTS

LXX 963 is dated to the $2^{nd}$ century. Sections are currently located at the Chester Beatty Library (P. Ch. Beatty VI) in Dublin, and the University of Michigan (P. Mich. Inv. 5554) in Ann Arbor.

# ALTERNATIVE SOURCES

The following is a list of alternative translations that were used for comparative analysis. Both the Peshitta and Coptic translations are believed to have been heavily based on the Septuagint, although do inherit relics of older Imperial Aramaic translations, or imports from the Hebrew translation.

The Aleppo Codex is dated to circa 920 CE. For centuries, it was housed at the Central Synagogue of Aleppo, from which its name is derived. It was the oldest known complete copy of the Hebrew scriptures used within Judaism until 1947, when it was seized and divided among Jewish families during anti-Jewish riots in Aleppo. The sections that have resurfaced are currently at the Israel Museum in Jerusalem. Approximately 40% is still missing. *Deuteronomy* chapters 32 through 34 are at the Israel Museum.

The Leningrad Codex is dated to 1008 (or 1009) AD. It is currently located at the National Library of Russia (Firkovich B 19 A) in St. Petersburg. The Leningrad Codex is the oldest complete copy of the Hebrew scriptures used within Judaism.

The Peshitta is the Syriac translation of the Christian bible. The Old Testament was translated from older Aramaic and Hebrew sources during the late $2^{nd}$ century CE, however, later redacted to become more similar to the Septuagint in the $5^{th}$ century.

The Targum Onkelos is generally accepted as having been compiled by Aquila (Onkelos) of Sinope between 100 and 120 CE, although the surviving copies are all in Babylonian Aramaic, and the text appears to have been updated linguistically in Babylon in the $4^{th}$ or $5^{th}$ centuries CE. Some scholars believe Aquila was reworking a now lost, older Judean-Aramaic targum from the $1^{st}$ century. The Megillah (3a) tractate of the Babylonian Torah claims that the Onkelos Targum is a restoration of a version of the Torah in use before the time of Ezra the scribe in the $4^{th}$ century BCE. While the idea that Aquila and Onkelos were the same person is debated, the Talmuds mention both of them doing the same thing, creating a targum in the same era, but do not confirm they are the same person. Therefore, the Onkelos is sometimes viewed as being a continuation of an older Babylonian Aramaic translation from the Neo-Babylonian, Persian, or Greek eras.

The Targum Pseudo-Jonathan has historically been misidentified as the Targum Jonathan, and is commonly called the Targum Pseudo-Jonathan in academic literature. Its oldest name is the Targum Pseudo-Jonathan, which is used here. It is written in Palestinian-Aramaic, and generally dated to sometime between the 4$^{th}$ and 11$^{th}$ centuries. Some scholars believe it originated in the 4$^{th}$ century, and was modified after the Islamic conquest of Palestine, as it includes some Arabic names generally found in Islamic sources. It existed before the crusades, as it was documented at the time.

The Targum Jerusalem is a collection of fragments from one or more targums written in Judean Aramaic that surfaced in Italy during the medieval era. It contains a number of heretical concepts, such as Judean-polytheism, suggesting some fragments are relics of a polytheist Israelite sect from before the Maccabean Revolt. The oldest Targum Jerusalem fragments date to the medieval period or later, and are copies of a manuscript reworked in the 5$^{th}$ century CE. However, the Targum is written in a form of Judeo-Aramaic that supports its origin in the Persian, Hellenistic, or Hasmonean eras. It has also been labeled as the Jerusalem Targum in some literature due to the dialect, or the Targum Jerusalem.

The Vetus Latina are the old Latin translations of the Septuagint and other Israelite texts that predate Jerome's Latin Orthodox Bible in the 5$^{th}$ century. Some of the texts appear to have been translated directly from Aramaic or Hebrew source texts, however, most appear to have been translations from the Greek translations.

# ALTERNATIVE SOURCES

The Codex Lugdunensis (VL 100) is composed of two manuscripts: 403 and 1964 which are dated to between 550 and 600 CE. They are currently located at the Bibliothèque de la Ville in Lyon.

The Munich Palimpsest (VL 104) is dated to circa 650 CE. It is currently located at the Bavarian State Library in Munich.

The Codex Gothicus Legionensis (VL 91) is a 10th century Vulgate manuscript currently located at the Basilica of San Isidoro, in León. The original Vulgate was the Latin translation created by Jerome in the 5th century. Jerome's translation used both the Greek and Hebrew text for sources. It was used along side the Vetus Latina texts in Latin speaking regions until the Roman Catholic church adopted a formal form of it in 1590 known as the Sixtine Vulgate.

Sahidic manuscripts are translations of the Septuagint into Sahidic (also known as Thebaic), one of the six dialects of Coptic, the classical era form of the Egyptian language. Sahidic was the dominant form of Coptic used before the 11th century, and is believed to have originated in the region around Hermopolis, at the boundary between Upper and Lower Egypt. Translations of the Septuagint into Sahidic are known to have existed by the 4th century, however, early non-dialect specific translations are generally accepted as having been made as early as the 1st century CE, with some scholars suggesting the 1st century BCE. The early non-dialect specific forms of Coptic are generally grouped with Sahidic, as Sahidic did not have a standardized spelling until the 6th century.

Sahidic manuscript 17 is dated to the 4th century. It is currently located at the British Library (Or. 7594) in London.

Sahidic manuscript 296L is dated to the 11th century. It is currently located at the Staatliche Museen zu Berlin Preußischer Kulturbesitz (P. 8770) in Berlin, the Bibliothèque nationale de France (Copte 129 and 132) in Paris, the British Library (Or. 3579 A) in London, the Österreichische Nationalbibliothek (K 9682, K 9691, K 9699, K 9702) in Vienna.

Sahidic manuscript 2001 is dated to the 4<sup>th</sup> century. It is currently located at the Chester Beatty Library (Cpt 2039) in Dublin, and the Bibliotheca Bodmeriana (Papyrus Bodmer XVIII) in Cologny.

Sahidic manuscript 2006 is dated to the 9<sup>th</sup> or 10<sup>th</sup> century. It is currently located at the Morgan Library & Museum (M 566) in New York.

Sahidic manuscript 2044 is dated to the 7<sup>th</sup> century. It is currently located at the Institut Français d'Archéologie Orientale (Inv. no. 215A) in Cairo, the Bibliothèque nationale de France (Copte 129, Copte 132, Copte 133) in Paris, Bibliothèque nationale et universitaire (Copte 27) in Strasbourg, the British Library (Or. 3579 A) in London, the Österreichische Nationalbibliothek (K 2596, K 2861, K 9384, K 9849, K 20769, K 20770) in Vienna, the University Library (P. Mich. Inv. No. 4696,40) in Ann Arbor, the Morgan Library & Museum (M 664 B) in New York, and the Biblioteca Apostolica Vaticana (Borg. copt. 109, cass. III, fasc. 6) in Vatican City.

Sahidic manuscript 2048 is dated to the 9<sup>th</sup> or 10<sup>th</sup> century. It is currently located at the Bibliothèque nationale de France (Copte 129) in Paris, the Musée du Louvre (E 10006, E 10077, E10080, R 241) de Paris, the Bibliothèque nationale et universitaire (Copte 264, frg. 1) in Strasbourg, the Österreichische Nationalbibliothek (K 9767, K 9809) in Vienna, and the Biblioteca Apostolica Vaticana (Borg. copt. 109, cass. IV, fasc. 10) in Vatican City.

Sahidic manuscript 2178L is dated to between 927 and 940 CE. It is currently located at the Bibliothèque nationale de France (Copte 129, Copte 132, Copte 133) in Paris, and the University Library (Add. 1876) in Cambridge.

# ALTERNATIVE SOURCES

Bohairic manuscripts are translations of the Septuagint into Bohairic (also known as Memphitic), one of the six dialects of Coptic, the classical era form of the Egyptian language. These dialects were written slightly differently, and therefore words transliterated into Coptic retain slightly different pronunciations, reflecting the different source texts used. Bohairic originated in the western Nile Delta of northern Egypt. The earliest Bohairic manuscripts date to the 4th century, however, the majority of texts come from the 9th century or later. Bohairic is the dialect used today as the liturgical language of the Coptic Orthodox Church, although Sahidic was used before the 11th century. Translations of the Septuagint were made into at least five of the Coptic dialects, however, complete copies only survive in Bohairic and Sahidic.

# DEAD SEA SCROLLS

The following is a list of the Dead Sea Scrolls mentioned in the notes for this book. Most are held by the Israel Museum in Jerusalem.

DSS 1Q4 (1QDeut$^a$) is dated to the Roman era in Judea and Palestine (6 to 390 AD).

DSS 1Q5 (1QDeut$^b$) is dated to the Roman era in Judea and Palestine (6 to 390 AD).

DSS 4Q28 (4QDeut$^a$) is dated to the Maccabees Revolt in Judea (165 to 140 BC).

DSS 4Q29 (4QDeut$^b$) is dated to the early Hasmonean dynasty of Judea (140 to 100 BC).

DSS 4Q30 (4QDeut$^c$) is dated to the early Hasmonean dynasty of Judea (140 to 100 BC).

DSS 4Q31 (4QDeut$^d$) is dated to the middle Hasmonean dynasty of Judea (100 to 50 BC).

DSS 4Q32 (4QDeut$^e$) is dated to the late Hasmonean dynasty of Judea (50 to 40 BC).

DSS 4Q33 (4QDeut$^f$) is dated to the late Hasmonean dynasty of Judea, circa 50 BC.

DSS 4Q34 (4QDeut$^g$) is dated to the late Herodian dynasty of Judea, or the early Roman rule of Judea (1 to 25 AD).

DSS 4Q35 (4QDeut$^h$) is dated to approximately the transition from the Hasmonean to Herodian dynasties of Judea, circa 37 BC.

DSS 4Q36 (4QDeut$^i$) is dated to the middle Hasmonean dynasty of Judea (100 to 50 BC).

DSS 4Q37 (4QDeut$^j$) is dated to the Roman rule of Judea, circa 50 AD.

DSS 4Q38 (4QDeut$^{k1}$) is dated to the Herodian dynasty in Judea (37 BC to 6 AD).

DSS 4Q38a (4QDeut$^{k2}$) is dated to the Herodian dynasty in Judea (37 BC to 6 AD).

DSS 4Q39 (4QDeut$^l$) is dated to the late Hasmonean dynasty of Judea, circa 50 BC.

DSS 4Q40 (4QDeut$^m$) is dated to approximately the transition from the Hasmonean to Herodian dynasties of Judea, circa 37 BC.

DSS 4Q41 (4QDeut$^n$) is dated to the Herodian dynasty in Judea (37 BC to 6 AD).

DSS 4Q42 (4QDeut$^o$) is dated to the late Hasmonean dynasty of Judea (75 to 37 BC).

DSS 4Q43 (4QDeut$^p$) is dated to the late Hasmonean dynasty of Judea (75 to 37 BC).

DSS 4Q44 (4QDeut$^q$) is dated to approximately the transition from the Hasmonean to Herodian dynasties of Judea, circa 37 BC.

DSS 4Q45 (4QpaleoDeut$^r$) is dated to the late Hasmonean dynasty of Judea (100 to 37 BC).

DSS 5Q1 (5QDeut) is dated to the Maccabees Revolt in Judea (165 to 140 BC).

# SHAPIRA SCROLLS

The Shapira scrolls, also known as the Shapira manuscript or Moabite Deuteronomy, are a collection of leather strips supposedly discovered in the Arnon valley of modern Jordan in the 1860s. While they were initially accepted as authentic by the Jewish antiquities dealer Moses Shapira, they were later discredited as forgeries by both German and British biblical scholars. Since the discovery of the Dead Sea scrolls in the 1940s, there have been several scholars who have called into question the claims that the scrolls were a forgery, however, their whereabouts is unknown, and therefore no modern analysis of the leather scrolls is possible.

Several reasons were given for the initial claims that the scrolls were a forgery, including the script, language, and content. The script is a form of Phoenician, similar to the Moabite script of the 800s BC, however, the language includes Imperial Aramaic terms not used until the Persian era, several centuries later. The content is not a match for any surviving translation of *Deuteronomy*, however, does include many parallel statements. Some of the statements are somewhat heretical, however, do seem similar to the beliefs of the Hasidian sect of Judahites reported to have been living in the region under Greek rule between 330 and 240 BC.

Moses Shapira had previously been involved in discovery and authentication of both authentic and fraudulent artifacts for the museums and universities of Europe, including 1700 fake Moabite artifacts that the Berlin museum bought. After German and British scholars reported the scrolls were a forgery, Shapira fled to the Netherlands, where he continued to claim the scrolls were authentic until killing himself several weeks later. The leather strips were subsequently sold at Sothby's a couple of years later, before disappearing.

While the leather was reported to have looked very old, the idea that it could be thousands of years old was dismissed until the discovery of the Dead Sea scrolls in a similar climate in the 1940s. The scrolls are included in this analysis, however, it is not clear that the scrolls weren't forged in the 1860s. If the manuscript was not forged in the 1860s, it was probably the remains of a Torah used by either the Hasidian or Tobian Judahite sects during the Greek era, both of which were reported to have been living in the region.

# ALSO AVAILABLE

# ALSO AVAILABLE

- Septuagint: History, Volume 2

- Octateuch: The Original Orit

ENOCH AND METATRON SERIES:
- Books of Enoch Collection

- Books of Enoch and Metatron Collection

- Books of Metatron Collection

- Secrets of Enoch

OTHER TRANSLATIONS:
- Apocalypses of Ezra

- Arabic Maccabees

- Hebrew Maccabees

- Life of Adam and Eve

- Memories of the New Kingdom

- Septuagint's Esther and the Vetus Latina Esther

- Septuagint's Ezekiel and the Ba'al Cycle

- Septuagint's Job and the Testament of Job

- Septuagint's Proverbs and the Wisdom of Amenemope

- The Amarna Letters

- Testaments of the Patriarchs Collection

- Tobit and Ahikar

- Ugaritic Texts: Ba'al Cycle

- Wisdom of Ahikar